WHODUNIT MYSTERIES

WHODUNIT MYSTERIES

PIT YOUR WITS AGAINST OUR TEAM OF SLEUTHS TO SOLVE THE CASES

TIM DEDOPULOS

ARCTURUS

ARCTURUS

This edition published in 2016 by Arcturus Publishing Limited
26/27 Bickels Yard, 151–153 Bermondsey Street,
London SE1 3HA

Copyright © Arcturus Holdings Limited

ISBN: 978-1-78599-011-3
AD004831NT

Illustrations by David Mostyn

Printed in China

Contents

INTRODUCTION

We have very curious natures, we humans. In fact, it's one of our greatest strengths. The need to understand is one of the things that makes us who we are. If our ancestors had been happy with "it just is", there would have been no scientific advancement, no technology, none of the things that we take for granted in the modern world. That facility to wonder—and imagine, and test—has allowed us to become who we are. It's difficult even to imagine a version of humanity without its curiosity.

Nowadays, though, the drive to solve problems in a satisfying way is a surprisingly tricky itch to scratch. For most of us, the answer to anything we might wonder is one quick internet search away, or else so far beyond everyday solution that it might as well be meaningless. If someone among the general public knows the answer, it's on the web. If not, you probably need several

Inspector Parnacki

academic degrees and a million-dollar lab to even begin trying to work it out.

That's where puzzles come in. Solving problems for fun has been a common pastime for as long as we have records. Even in the most ancient shards of human civilization, back in the earliest days of Babylonia, we find riddles and conundrums. They're there in every society we know of, present and past. That problem-solving urge is universal. It's part of what makes us who we are. Happily, doing puzzles isn't just fun, it's also very good for the brain. Mental exercise is now proven to help keep your memory and deductive ability intact.

The puzzles in this book will, I hope, entertain you, and give your deductive abilities a bit of a work-out. Each one depicts a crime, and your task is to spot who did it. In the first section, Level 1, the flaws of logic that identify the guilty parties are fairly straightforward. They won't all be easy to spot, but events

Miss Mary Miller

should be relatively tangle-free. In Level 2 puzzles, events are a little more opaque, and the evidence somewhat less clear-cut. Hints are there to help you, however, if you decide that you need them.

You'll be guided in your enquiries by three unusually perceptive investigators. **Inspector Parnacki** is known to the press as "Paddington" because of some high-profile work in that area of London, England, earlier in his career. Now he is the pride of his new home city's police force. Impeccably dressed, with manners to match, he's as insightful as he is logical. **Miss Mary Miller** is a passionate ornithologist, socialite, and tea-drinker. Advancing age has not dulled her spectacular powers of observation one whit, and although she appears kindly and innocuous, she has a mind like a steel trap. Then there's **Joshua Cole**, an ambitious young journalist with perfect recall who works for the *Sentinel*, one of the city's leading newspapers. He'll do whatever is required to get to the heart of the story he's after. This formidable trio will be your companions as you work your way through the cases in this book.

Happy puzzling!
Tim Dedopulos

Joshua Cole

Cases

The Intruder

Sigmund Huydgins had been murdered in his lounge, killed by a single knife-thrust to the neck. He was found in his usual arm-chair. This faced the fire, and sat in front of a pair of tall French windows which offered a doorway out onto a pleasant-looking patio—or at least they had until they were painted shut. The garden beyond was a little unkempt, October leaves scattered across it. The room showed no signs of disturbance or struggle. Nothing had been stolen, as far as the family could tell. The murder weapon, of a common style used in leather and craft work, had been left in the wound, and offered no useful leads.

Inspector Parnacki looked out at the grounds thoughtfully. Huydgins had been ill for a decade or more, and cantankerous with it. His wife, Delpha, had committed suicide four years previously, and the case notes implied that her husband's ire had been a major contributor to her despair. Hearing footsteps, Parnacki turned round.

Officer Sullivan entered the room. "The family are ready for you, Inspector," he said.

"Thank you, John." Parnacki followed Sullivan back through the house to the small reception room that had been set aside for the initial interviews. He took out his notepad. "Would you bring in the nurse first?"

Lora Ball was in her thirties. She appeared pleasant, in an

institutional sort of way, and was tidily dressed in a mix of blue and white cottons. "I've been full-time here for seven years," she explained. "Mr. H's attacks were quite frequent. I was with him

about fifty percent of the time, and lived in a small suite in the old servant's quarters. His family were never close, so after poor Mrs. H. died, I probably talked with him more than anyone else. He was difficult, yes, but really he was just sad, and in terrible pain. I was out visiting the pharmacy when it happened. By the time I got back, the police were here. I gather Scott found his father, and called them. I wish I could tell you more."

Jeff Huydgins was the victim's elder son. Sharply dressed, with a slightly predatory air, he seemed more annoyed than saddened by his loss. "I took over from Father almost 11 years ago, when he first became unwell. I like to think that the firm has prospered in that time. We weren't exactly close, no. He was always an angry man, and I was relieved to reach adulthood. I did my duty, though, and visited every weekend without fail. That's more than Scott or Barbie can claim. I was here yesterday morning, and spent a couple of hours with him—for all the good it did either of us. Miss Ball had gone out by the time I left. I went straight to my club, for a stiff scotch and soda, and from there to home."

Huydgins's daughter, Barbara Rodgers, was between her brothers in age. Although she looked fit and tanned, her face was strongly marked with lines of old pain. "My husband Delroy and I were hiking with our boys all yesterday," she said, with a defiant air. "We made our way up through the Penton woods to the top of Hangman's Mount, and had a picnic there. It was very pleasant. I'm sad that the boys have lost their grandfather, I suppose, but I hope Mother can rest a little more easily now. Distressed? Lord forgive me, no, of course I'm not distressed. He was a horrible father, particularly for a shy girl. I won't miss him."

Scott Huydgins, the youngest son, was thirty-seven. Tidy and crisp, he seemed subdued. "I found him, yes," he said. "Terrible thing. I arrived about two. I try to come by on Saturdays, whenever I can. Jeff was already gone, and Miss Ball was out, so I let myself in. I thought he'd be dozing. Father was an old terror, but it was horrible to see him like that. I should have realized something was wrong when I pulled up in the drive and saw the lounge windows open. Father hated draughts. I'm afraid I closed them without thinking. Then I called for help, and waited for your people to arrive. I wouldn't say I'm *sad* exactly, but for better or worse, he was a central force in all our lives, and it'll be odd not to have him there as a focus."

Once the interviews were done, Parnacki closed his notepad, and nodded briskly to Officer Sullivan. "Let's get the killer down to the station, shall we?"

Whom does Parnacki suspect, and why?

HINT

PAINT

The Bowers Murder

The Bowers murder was big news. Furman Bowers, an influential banker, had been executed in front of his open safe. The *Chronicle* had broken the initial murder, the *Tribune* had managed to get the first interview with the widow, and at the *Sentinel*, the editor was incandescent. Josh Cole stoically endured the abuse the man hurled at him, and left his office with the editor's final words ringing in his ears. "Get me a scoop, boy, or I'll turn your twitching corpse into our own big lead story!"

Josh closed the office door, and the whole newsroom turned to look at him with expressions ranging from sympathetic to maliciously amused. Ignoring them all, he grabbed his coat and notebook, and headed to the lifts.

His first stop was at Glinton and Mathers, attorneys-at-law. Furman Bowers' family lawyer, Darrell Dalton, had worked there for eight years. A small, fidgety man, Dalton took no pains to hide his disappointment when Josh turned out to be a reporter rather than a potential new client, but grudgingly answered a few questions just to get rid of him. "Yes, Mr. Cole, my client was having some temporary difficulties. No, I will absolutely not share any details, on or off record. No, he had not received any threats, death or otherwise. No, he had no enemies, whatever that even means. Suggestions that he was involved in anything shady are pure fabrications. To the best of my knowledge, Mr. Furman hadn't even heard of Benny Lucas. No, I have most certainly *never* met Mr. Lucas or any of his representatives. Mr. Furman was an upstanding member of the business community and had no truck with organized crime. Now, if you'll please excuse me, I have work to do."

Ruth Bowers, Furman's wife, was more forthcoming. She welcomed Josh in, poured him a coffee, and talked freely and movingly about her loss. "He was a sweet, gentle man," she said.

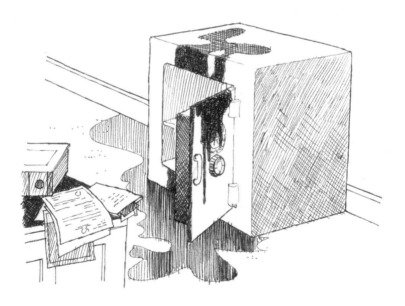

"I loved him very much. But he could be stubborn. I'm sure the assassins had to torture the safe combination out of him. That's probably why they killed him afterwards. Oh, I wish they'd seized me instead! I'd have just told them the combination, rather than force them into brutality and rage, and then we'd still be together. It's so senseless. Poor Furman said something about a Mr. Lucas the other night—some bad sort, I felt—but I didn't pay close attention."

Two other people had been around the house that morning. One was the gardener, Charles Hedrick, who worked there three times a week. A hardy, knotted old man, he was actively hostile. "I'm sick of you newsies, poking and prying," he declared. "So what if it was one of the shotguns from the shed what did him? They're not mine, and it's not locked. I was working on the drainage in the south lawns, all damned day. I didn't even hear it. First I knew was the police bossing me around. I don't care if you're just doing your job, Mister whoever you are, you're spoiling my lunch."

The other person who had visited the house was a deliveryman named Richard Kitts, who had been there to drop off some logs. "Yeah, I went there, filled up his wood box, gave the missus the invoice, and then I left again. I was only there two minutes, and you can go ask the folks on my round before and after what time I was with *them*. I didn't see nothing. No, I never heard of no Benny Lucas. What? Sure you said his first name, how else would I know it? No, I don't have no record. Where did you hear that? Rubbish. Complete lies. You print that and I'll kick your shiny head in, buster, and that's a promise. Then I'll have some lawyer sue whatever's left."

Wearily, Josh headed back to the office. The Bowers file stared at him balefully. As stories went, "A Widow's Grief" wasn't going to cut it. He flicked through the crime-scene photos that his police contact had given to him—and every other journo on the story, dammit. Furman's body had been removed before they'd been taken. The safe was wide open and completely cleaned out, the bare metal gleaming. Blood soaked the floor and the wall around it, and almost entirely hid the maker's name on the front of the heavy door. The carpet was just a sea of mess. The corner of an untidy desk in the foreground took up a chunk of the picture. It was covered in papers, files and ledgers.

He leapt to his feet, and dashed to the editor's office, barging straight in. "I've got it," he told his startled boss. "I know who killed Bowers!"

What has Josh noticed?

HINT
PHOTOS

A Vexing Theft

Mary Miller let her friend pour her a strong cup of tea, then patted her on the arm. "Please do tell me what happened, my dear."

Sighing, Eldora Watson glanced down at her own teacup. "The Etruscan necklace was stolen last night, during the storm. Thieves were prowling around while I was in the next room! It's horrifying!"

"Terrible. Is the Etruscan the one with the sapphires?"

"That's it. Matthews discovered the theft late last night, and woke me up. Whoever it was broke the library window— smearing mud all over the carpet—and took the necklace from its case. They obviously knew where it was. Nothing else was disturbed. I suppose I should be grateful I wasn't injured."

"And you didn't hear anything?" Miss Miller asked.

"No. But between the downpour and the thunder, I'm not that surprised. It's most distressing."

Miss Miller took a slow sip of her tea. "What time did you retire?"

"Yesterday afternoon was the James-Heaton wedding. It was lovely, but quite tiring, and all that thunder strained my nerves. I went to bed at about 10pm, when the storm was finally clearing, and I was out like a light. It never occurred to me to check in the library. Why would it?"

"Why, indeed. What about your staff?"

"Well, Alfreda worked until 9.30pm, and then she went out to meet friends. She didn't get in until the morning, but that's fine, I knew she'd be out. Matthews is typically up until around 11pm. He was doing his final rounds when he found that the necklace had been stolen. Mrs. Beasley leaves after dinner is served every evening, at 7pm. Then there's Mr. Rolen and his boy, Merritt Smith. They sleep in the gatehouse rather than up here. I've spoken to Mr. Rolen. He said, as best I can quote, 'Not a soul trod the drive between the end of that rain and the ladies returning after seven this morning, but the devil hisself could have driven a herd of tigers up there during that deluge, and I'd be none the wiser.' He meant Mrs. Beasley and Alfreda, of course, who got in at the same time." She paused.

"Do tigers even herd?"

"They're solitary creatures, but I believe the fashionable term of venery is 'an ambush of tigers'. Your gardener sounds like a fanciful fellow."

"That he is," Eldora agreed. "Makes him quite the wizard with a flowerbed."

"Yes, he's very good." Miss Miller smiled. "Now, perhaps I should have a little look in the library."

"Of course. We haven't cleaned

in there, you understand. The police asked me to leave it as it was."

Miss Miller nodded, and the two ladies went across to the library. One pair of windows stood half-open, a shattered pane clearly visible at the bottom of the left-hand frame. The latch was flipped up carelessly. Mud was smeared in a thick line from the window to the necklace's case. The thief had been careful to avoid visible footprints, opting instead to leave long, dragged streaks. Water had leeched out of the mud deposits, staining the delicately pale carpet, obvious against the pristine condition of the rest of the floor. The case itself had been flipped open. Apart from the initial shattering of the glass, it would have been a quiet theft.

When she got closer, Miss Miller could make out a few smears of mud on the windowsill itself. Apart from those, the sill was spotless. Just outside, the ground was churned up, but no clear footprints were visible. The windows were opened about half-way, more than wide enough for a man—or a woman—to get through. There was a stretch of unmarked carpet, and then the mud smears began.

Miss Miller backed away from the smears again to stand next to a tall case of books. "My dear Eldora, I'm afraid I know the identity of your thief."

Who does Miss Miller suspect, and why?

HINT

STORM

Attack Among the Antiques

The owner of an antique store, Hiram Beauchamp, had been attacked by a masked assailant on Tuesday night. Just two days beforehand, Beauchamp had attended a large annual auction of orphaned goods, the Summer Sell-Off, and purchased a significant amount of stock. A number of small, valuable pieces had been stolen from his stock rooms and shop floor, and Beauchamp himself had received a nasty blow to the head. Earlier in the day, Parnacki visited his hospital bed to conduct an initial interview.

"He was a big guy," Beauchamp had told him. "Taller than me. Broad in the shoulder. Muscular, you know the type. Like a navvy. He came at me. I'd just turned the main light off. I didn't get a great look. He was masked anyway. Some mesh flattening his face. Tight black clothing. I grabbed a poker, and swung it at him good. He just blocked it with his forearm. Smacked me straight out with a cosh. I woke up here. There doesn't seem to be any brain damage. Nose is mashed, though. Docs say I'm lucky. I believe 'em. Hope you can get this guy, Inspector. He's a brute."

The responding officers had canvassed the area around the store and come up with a shortlist of four suspects who'd had the opportunity for the crime for Inspector Parnacki to interview. He decided to start his interviews by talking to Gordon Henderson, Beauchamp's current assistant.

When Henderson entered the interview room, he was wearing

smart trousers and a starched shirt, open at the collar, with the
sleeves rolled up. He looked downcast and worried. Henderson
was no taller than Hiram Beauchamp himself, maybe 5 feet 7
inches, and slender. "Is Hiram OK?" he asked Parnacki urgently.
The inspector nodded, and Henderson relaxed immediately.
"Thank God," he said. "I suppose you want to know about my

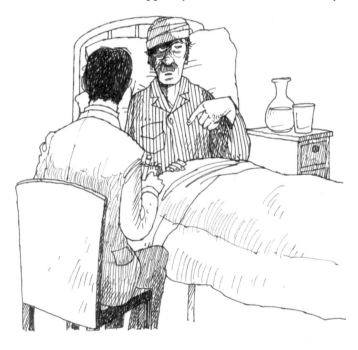

movements last night. I finish work at 5.30, and yesterday I went straight home. Becky and I—she's my wife—had dinner with our friends next door. We were there until 9pm. I understand you have to talk to everyone, but I hope you can let me out soon. Becky will worry."

Mack Gerber was Beauchamp's assistant before Henderson. Like most of the suspects, he was a tall, meaty man. He was wearing jeans, and a dark leather jacket over a button-down shirt. "I worked for old Hiram for a few months," he said. He looked hot. "It was okay, but the work was real boring, you know? Truth is, I'm not real interested in old stuff. I tried to tough it out, but I ended up getting too sick of it. My girl, she don't like it if I quit a job, so I got Hiram to fire me instead. I was out on the town last night, met up with a couple of the boys, had some drinks. They'll vouch for me."

Local workman Chas Matheson was of a build with Gerber. He had a sullen face, and short, almost military hair. He was wearing a light, short-sleeved shirt and pair of slacks. "Yeah, I know the old man you mean," he said. "I never been into his shop, though. Not my sort of scene, a place like that. My room comes with enough furniture and bad old pictures. I finished at six, and went out, got some food at the Tavern, then went and hit some bars. That's about it. No, I don't really remember where I ended up. I had a couple at the Tavern, which is less than a block from the old man's place, then I just went wandering. I do that sometimes. I stopped in at a couple of places that I didn't know. You gotta try new stuff, right?"

The final suspect, Wayman Suttles, had a history of petty theft and mugging. He could be found most nights at the same bar Matheson had mentioned, the Tavern. He too was strongly muscled, and over 6 feet in height. He was wearing cut-off trousers and a sleeveless vest, along with an expression of impatient annoyance. "What is it this time, Paddington?" he demanded. "Does the famous inspector need to fill up some quota, maybe? Tick off your 'hassle Suttles' box for the quarter? I didn't do nothing to nobody or nowhere, and that's official. Last night? I was in the Tavern, just like you know. I got there about five, and I didn't budge until they closed. Lila was working the bar, she'll tell you all about it, her and a dozen other regulars. So charge me or let me go, eh? It's boiling in here."

Parnacki came out of the interview room, and nodded to the duty sergeant. "We can let three of these men go right away," he said.

Who does Parnacki suspect, and why?

HINT
THE SEASON

The Killing of Rachael Wightman

The murder of a pretty young schoolmistress was always going to be big news, particularly when she had been popular, vivacious, and the niece (once removed) of one of the Mayor's senior aides. Her death had dominated the front pages so completely that the day's other two main stories, the new wolf enclosure at the zoo and the unannounced bus strike, had barely received a mention.

Josh Cole sat at his desk in the newsroom, trying to find a fresh angle for another story on Rachael Wightman's killing. The odd, slightly ritualistic way in which her body had been posed was already old news. There was little to say about her tragic death that hadn't already been said.

The police were pursuing a short list of primary suspects, but it was far too soon to risk talking about them in print. Some bridges were just too important to risk burning, and anyway, discussing a short-list of suspects was a great way to get sued.

Thad Cable was a builder. He'd been working on the house next door to the Wightmans' for a couple of weeks. He openly admitted to having noticed Miss Wightman, and to finding her uncommonly attractive, but that was hardly uncommon. A friend of Cable's had characterized him as having a bit of a temper, but that was meaningless. According to the man himself, he'd been away from the work-site having lunch with his wife, Imogen, and her family. Imogen Cable had been only too happy to confirm that Thad had been with her, apparently. Even so, the police were still considering him as a possibility.

The second suspect, Irvin Ingram, was Rachael's cousin. He was known to have visited the victim the previous evening, so was a suspect primarily by proximity. A cousin on her father's side, he had no connection to any city politicians, which automatically made him less intriguing journalistically, and he worked as a secretary in a financial office. The police report clearly didn't find him particularly interesting. During the hour or so between Rachael's last known movements and the discovery of her body, he'd been stuck in traffic, on a bus heading downtown, in order to fetch some reports that his boss required urgently from the bank that the firm was allied to.

The final suspect, Will Blazer, had the most potential to be the murderer. An acquaintance of Rachael's, he had fallen deeply in love with her, and had repeatedly attempted to pursue her. Although he had failed entirely to endear himself to the victim and had been gently but constantly rebuffed, he had broken down upon hearing of her death; according to the police reports, he consistently referred to her as the love of his life. It certainly seemed as if Mr. Blazer and reality were not on entirely close terms. He worked as an insurance salesman, and claimed to have been in a long sales meeting all that lunchtime.

Josh frowned as a detail hit him, and then started scribbling. If he timed his call to the police carefully, the *Sentinel* would be the only paper covering the murder arrest the following morning.

Who had Josh identified as the killer, and why?

HINTS
NEWS

The Thief of Time

From outside, there was nothing to show that a robbery had taken place. Farr's Fine Clocks was a tidy-looking shop on an unremarkable street, sandwiched between a furniture store and a reasonably upscale French-style delicatessen. A selection of decorative clocks of various sizes stood in the window. Inspector Parnacki studied the display for a moment. The clocks were all very close together in time, putting it at about ten minutes past four.

He entered the shop. The interior was as orderly as the window had suggested. Here too, the clocks were well-synchronized; not a trivial task.

"Can I help you?" The speaker was a small, neat man with a piercing gaze.

Parnacki nodded. "Bradley Farr, I assume? Inspector Parnacki."

The man smiled, bobbed his head a little. There was a long, nasty bruise on the back of his head. "Ah, Inspector. Good of you to come. Shall we talk in my workshop?" He gestured to a door behind him.

"That would be fine," Parnacki said, and followed Farr through a door beside the shop's glass service counter.

They walked into a smaller room. The walls were completely covered by sets of shelves, rows of little drawers, and similar compartments. Leather-topped desks stood beneath these, each with multiple lamps and large, arm-mounted magnifying glasses. A young, smartly attired woman looked up from a freestanding table which held several stacks of documents. She blinked at the inspector, and muttered something that sounded a lot like "Paddington Parnacki!"

Farr smiled at her perfunctorily. "Would you mind the shop for a little while, Minnie?"

She blushed. "Of course, Mr. Farr." She rose, and went into the shop, closing the door behind her.

"Would you like some coffee, Inspector? I can get Minnie to make some."

"No, thank you," Parnacki said.

Farr nodded. "Of course." He pulled a chair from one desk for Parnacki to sit on, then seated himself on another. "Where should we start?"

"According to my reports, you were assaulted, and forced to open your own safe. The contents were then stolen, including your payroll. Is that correct?"

"Yes," Farr said. "I was working here, on a mechanism, some time after 12.45. I heard a step behind me, but didn't think twice about it. Then there was a blast of pain, and I became disorientated and quite confused. When I came back to myself, I'd been firmly tied down to my chair, and I had a hood over my head. I have the rope and bag they used, if you need to examine them. A silly voice told me that if I behaved myself, and obeyed instructions, I would come to no further harm."

Parnacki blinked. "A silly voice?"

"Yes. Whoever it was had decided to speak in a squeaky falsetto, I assume to prevent recognition. I'm about 90 percent sure it was a man, but I can't even be perfectly certain about that. When you add in the fact that the payroll is only in the safe for about four hours a week, it makes me sure it was one of the staff."

"Disguising the voice does suggest that you'd recognize the speaker otherwise," said the inspector. "What next?"

"Well, I obeyed, of course," Farr said. "I didn't call for help, I listed the contents of the safe, informed the thief of the value of a couple of items in the shop which ultimately he decided not to take, and then opened the safe as requested. That's it there, above the shelf of casings just to your left. The thief rustled around for a little while, and then departed. It took me quite a lot of effort, but eventually I managed to worm my way out of my bonds. When I finally escaped, it was precisely two minutes to one thirty."

"I see," Parnacki said. "Were you alone in the shop?"

"Yes. Minnie is my secretary and assistant. Minnie Burgin. She says she was at lunch with her boyfriend, Enzo. Lawson Day tends the shop front, but he claims to be unwell today, and hasn't been to work. Finally there's Worth Herron, my new delivery man. He's only been with me for a couple of months, and he was out, supposedly delivering a carriage clock. Minnie, Lawson and Worth all know I go to the bank on Thursday mornings, and that I keep my more valuable supplies and equipment in there. Who knows what Minnie has told her young man. Any of them could have done it."

Parnacki nodded. "Thank you, Mr. Farr. You've been very helpful. I have a good idea of who the thief is."

Who does Parnacki suspect?

HINTS
PRACTICALITY

The Midwinter Ball

The church of St. Francis de Salle had been in a terrible state for years. Despite the efforts of the vicar's small, loyal congregation, funds for repair and renovation never quite seemed to arrive. It was too small, too out of the way. Eventually, Miss Miller's friend Frieda Boyer and her husband Clayton decided to intervene, and arranged a midwinter ball to raise money for improvements.

The ball was held at the Excelsior Hotel. The entire Riverside Suite had been given over to the event, and the staff had been warned to expect at least five hundred of the city's philanthropically inclined inhabitants. Miss Miller arrived at a little after 7pm, early enough to show Frieda that her support was serious, but not so early as to appear over-eager. The temperature outdoors was a few degrees below zero, and frost was already riming the hotel's ornamental ponds. She was very glad to get inside the hotel and receive a glass of hot punch.

The showcase of the ball was a selection of art from St. Francis de Salle. It contained paintings of the church from the last century, vibrant sketches of its stained glass windows, rubbings from its more interesting brasses, and, in pride of place, the church's relic—a simple-looking but valuable inkwell that had been used by the saint himself. The vicar stood nearby, hovering awkwardly as the great and the good murmured past. Miss Miller took pity on him, and engaged him in conversation about the church and the saint. Once over his initial discomfort, he proved to be an amusing and learned man.

A loud crash startled everyone, and several black-clad men in animal masks burst through the river-facing plate glass that served as the suite's outer wall. Freezing air accompanied them. One of them had a large pistol, and he fired it into the ceiling, silencing the screams. "Shut up," he shouted, his voice deep and rough. "Do what you're told, or die." He moved to the suite's door, and flipped the lock.

Two of the men rushed the showcase. The vicar stepped in front of the inkwell, and one of the pair casually smashed him out of the way with a forearm. They broke the case, and grabbed the relic. Meanwhile, three others were circulating among the crowd, taking necklaces, bracelets, wallets, and other valuables. Any protest was met with immediate violence.

After a couple of endless minutes, Miss Miller heard three clear blasts of a low-pitched whistle. Immediately the men withdrew, the gunman covering their retreat. Seconds later, they were gone. Higher-pitched whistles approaching quickly made it clear that the police were on their way.

Excusing herself from the traumatized vicar, Miss Miller moved to the window. There was no sign of the robbers, so she followed their path out of both the suite and the hotel grounds. Several police officers were just arriving, and she gave one a hurried explanation of events. The street was otherwise quiet, apart from an old beggar across the road, sheltering beside the riverside footpath. He was dressed in multiple layers of rags, and

had straggly hair and a matted beard. Even from 10 feet away, he stank of alcohol.

Two of the police officers went to talk to him, while several others made their way to the hotel. He spoke animatedly to the police, waving around a half-frozen bottle of scotch, but his voice was so slurred that it was difficult to know what he was saying to them. After a little time, one of the policemen took off down the riverside path at a swift pace, while the other sprinted back towards the main group.

Miss Miller stepped in front of the sprinting policeman, forcing him to a stop.

"Please excuse me, Madam," he managed. "A colleague will—"

"Arrest that beggar, officer," said Miss Miller, cutting in quietly but urgently. "He's not what he seems. He is with the thieves."

Why does Miss Miller suspect the beggar?

HINT

ICE

The Lost City

The explorer Collin Andrews had just returned from a long trip into the Sahara Desert, bearing news of an incredible discovery. After a short, fierce battle, the *Sentinel* managed to scoop an exclusive interview, and Josh Cole was sent to meet the man at his rooms at the Grand. Andrews was tall and fit, with a deeply tanned face, and despite some significant weathering, he remained handsome. There was a definite sense of his presence filling the room. While Josh's usual photographer, a sullen lad named Adam, stalked the room taking shots of the beaming explorer, Josh conducted his interview.

"Welcome back to civilization, Mr. Andrews."

Andrews grinned, white teeth gleaming in his nut-brown face. "Please, call me Collin. It's good to be home."

"Why don't you tell our readers a little about yourself?"

"I'm a local boy, you'll be glad to know. I've always been fascinated with the world, though. I spent some time in the merchant navy, and made friends and contacts across the globe. One of them invited me on an inland journey, to Kathmandu. I caught the exploration bug, and the rest is history. It's taken me from the temples of Cambodia to the depths of the Peruvian jungle and beyond. But I found something special this time."

"And what was that?"

"The ancient desert city of Irem, lost beneath the dunes for untold ages. There have been legends about the place for

centuries. Travellers would report a distant sighting of a spire where none could be, or a mirage of bits of wall that vanished almost as quickly as they appeared. The city is real, though, protected by a ring of forbidding hills. There is a way in, and inside, it's incredible. I found a whole city of strangely low-ceilinged buildings, so shallow I had to bend almost double at times. The temples were much taller, dominating all, and there were many statues of an unfamiliar god in the Egyptian form, something a little like a fat, sleek crocodile with a pronounced forehead and horns."

Josh jotted notes. "It sounds fascinating."

"It was. The Bedouin refuse to approach the area at all, insisting that it is a place of death. It might be that they vaguely remember stories of the city's fall. Certainly I came to no harm. Going without helpers meant that I had to abandon my non-essential supplies, but my word, it was worth it. I stayed as long as I dared, and took whatever notes I could, but it's a long, hard trip back out from the heart of the sands. Had I the food and water, I would have stayed a month within those decaying walls. I'll provide your editor with some sketches."

"What do you plan to do now?"

"Relax a little," Collin said, grinning again. "I think I've earned it. I landed back here last night on a little packet steamer, the *Valiant* out of Dunedin, and went straight to a barber to get a three-month thicket of hair and beard removed. Then I came here, to the Grand, and ordered the largest steak they had, and a bottle of champagne. We'll see what happens next."

"Wonderful," Josh said. "Thanks for your time, Collin. If I have any follow-up questions, I'll be in touch. It was a pleasure meeting you." He turned to the photographer, who was lurking against a wall at the back of the room. "Come on, Adam."

When he got back to the newsroom, he went to report to the editor.

"How did it go?" his boss asked.

"He's definitely a liar," Josh said. "He probably just spent a couple of months in Spain or Mexico, sitting on a beach and making up pretty stories."

Why does Josh think that?

HINT
FACILITIES

The Death of a Brother

"**I** just don't understand it, Mary." Nita York started crying again, and Miss Miller hugged her, patting her gently on the back. "Brad would never have taken his own life. Not the Brad I knew."

"I suppose we are sure that's what happened?"

"Yes, there's no doubt," Nita said. "Alfie—Alfie Rhea, Brad's best friend—got a call to go over there urgently. He hurried as quickly as he could, but as he got close to the front door, he spotted Brad through the attic window. As he watched, Brad kicked the stool away . . ." She started sobbing in earnest.

Miss Miller gave her a minute to regain her composure. "Alfie contacted the police?"

"Straight away. It was far too late, though. I'll miss him so much."

"I only met him a few times," Miss Miller said. "He seemed like a gentle fellow."

Nita nodded. "He was one of the kindest people I knew. Our parents had their faults, but they raised the pair of us to be decent and considerate. I just can't imagine him doing something so cruel and selfish, no matter how bad things were. It doesn't make any sense."

"Despair can do terrible things to a person," said Miss Miller gently.

"Of course, but why would he have been in despair and not mentioned it, not asked for help? Did he secretly hate me?"

"I know he didn't, Nita."

"Then why did he do this?"

Miss Miller sighed. "Well, I don't know. Did he have any serious problems?"

"Not really." She shrugged. "Not seriously serious. He was courting, a girl named Libby Norton, but that seemed to be going well enough. His work was wearying, he said. That's hardly enough to take your own life, though."

"No. Have you spoken to your mother?"

"A little. She was clearly in shock, and couldn't imagine why. No one can. Not Alfie, not Brad's boss, nobody."

"Is it possible that he'd had some sort of terrible medical news?"

Nita shuddered. "I suppose it's an outside possibility. Dr. Lloyd-Davies has looked after us both since we were born, though. He gave me a little something for my nerves yesterday, and I think he'd have at least alluded to it if there had been a problem."

"And Bradley gave no sign of any debility?"

"None. If he was in discomfort, he'd hardly have dragged a kitchen stool up three floors—as well as a ladder—just to kill himself in a dingy attic."

"No, I suppose not. Is it possible that there was a hidden side to his life?"

"That's what I keep asking myself. I can only imagine that the brother I knew was actually a mask, and there was some terrible darkness underneath that he kept hidden from all of us. It's horrible. Like losing him twice, if you see what I mean. Maybe he was mixed up in some dreadful criminal affair, or losing his mind, or some kind of terrible pervert who did unconscionable things."

Miss Miller patted Nita's hand. "I'm sure that wasn't the case, my dear. In fact, I very much doubt he killed himself at all."

Nita gasped. "What do you mean?"

Why does Miss Miller doubt that Bradley committed suicide?

HINT
ATTIC

$\mathcal{S}$tolen Sapphires

Walter Stoffle was well connected, so almost as soon as his wife discovered that an extremely valuable sapphire ring had been stolen, Inspector Parnacki was despatched to their home. On arriving, he was slightly surprised to discover that the day's party continued uninterrupted.

Mr. Stoffle, a serious-looking man in his fifties, answered the door, and took the inspector into a quiet drawing room. "Thank you for coming out so promptly," the man said. "I appreciate it. We give the staff Sundays off, so it's just us and our guests here today. I dislike imagining that one of our friends is a thief, but I can't see an alternative. So I haven't told anyone about the theft. My hope is that you can get it sorted out today, while we're all here, before anyone has a chance to make off with Fae's ring. It's insured of course, but it belonged to her grandmother."

"I'll do my best to help," Inspector Parnacki said, puffing at his pipe.

"Given your reputation, Inspector, I feel certain you'll solve this matter easily."

"You're too kind. First, let me ask, was there any time when one of your guests may have been alone?"

"Yes, sadly. We all split up after lunch for half an hour. I've been unwell, and I needed a little nap. Fae woke me up, and then we resumed, but I gather everyone else took the chance to do their own thing. That's when we discovered the theft, and decided to keep quiet for the moment. The ring was in a box on Fae's dresser. Someone must have crept into the room while I was asleep and taken it. The rest of the time, we've all been together, or at the very worst, in groups of two or three."

"I see."

Walter Stoffle nodded gravely. "I'm reasonably certain it was there before I went to sleep."

"Perhaps you could bring people in here for me to have a word with, Mr. Stoffle? Ideally one by one, without mentioning why?"

"Of course," Stoffle said.

"Let's start with Mrs. Stoffle," said Parnacki.

Walter blinked, and then nodded reluctantly.

Fae Stoffle was surprisingly collected, but there was a small spark of fury beneath her polite façade. "When Walter went for his snooze, I took the left-overs back to the kitchen, along with the plates. Mrs. Benton had left us a cold buffet, so I ensured that everything was put away properly, and rinsed the dishes. Then I sat down for a few moments, put some coffee on to start brewing, and went to wake him. That's when we discovered the theft."

Antoine Blanchard was a towering man, almost 6½ feet tall, and as thin as a rail. He spoke with a faint French accent. Like the other men, he was a banker in the city. "After lunch, I was practising my snooker game on Walter's table. It is something I do at every chance, in fact. There are just two things where too much skill is impossible, snooker and loveplay."

Una Blanchard was the youngest person in attendance by a good decade. She was quite lovely, and blushed deeply when the inspector asked about her movements after lunch. "Something I ate disagreed with me, I'm afraid. I was, ah, indisposed."

Joey Whitson bore a passing resemblance to Father Christmas, although his beard was gray rather than white, and somewhat better trimmed. "During lunch, I noticed the postman come past, and he appeared to stop at Walter's gate. So I wandered down to check whether there was any mail waiting. There wasn't anything though, so I strolled back up to the house. I'm not so fast on my feet any more."

Oda Whitson was tall and slender, with an air of elegant grace. "I was in the gardens behind the house. Fae's roses are always superb, particularly at this time of year. I quite lost track of time among them, I'm afraid. She had to call me back once everyone else had reassembled to continue the festivities."

Boyce Prowse, a tall man, appeared startled by the affair. "I went to look over Walter's collection of trophies after lunch," he said. "He's got a particularly savage-looking bear in his lodge room. Walter says he's most proud of the moose, but I must admit I'm not sure why. It's a big beast, but it's not stuffed very well, and a herbivore hardly seems like much challenge. Walter insists *it* nearly bagged *him*, though."

Deborah Prowse was small, and positively serene compared to her effusive husband. "I was reading, in here actually," she said, and pointed towards a paperback on a nearby table. "The Stoker novel, the one that was so popular a few years ago. I've not read it before. It's rather compelling. I was hoping Fae might lend it to me, but it seems gauche to ask now."

After the initial interviews had been conducted, Walter Stoffle returned to the inspector. "What would you like to do now?" he asked. "Is there any way I can help?"

"Actually," said Parnacki, "there is one person I would like to question more closely. A lot more closely, in fact."

Who does Parnacki suspect?

HINTS
WEEKEND

The Swaggerty Murder

S waggerty, Hawton & Smith was a firm well-known to all of the city's journalists. Most of the more persistent libel lawsuits came from their lavish offices on Haight Street. The murder of Hershel Swaggerty was about to be very big news, and Joshua Cole was the only journalist who knew about it yet. He'd left an initial breaking news piece with his editor, and was now frantically running around town trying to get material for a longer piece before it broke. Fortunately, the firm themselves were keeping quiet while the surviving partners prepared a statement.

Swaggerty's wife Harriet had been too distraught to speak, let alone give Josh anything useful. Adam, his photographer, had at least managed a quick snap that would play well. Harmon Sands, the junior partner under Swaggerty, had been more forthcoming, once Josh had promised to quote him as "an anonymous source."

"Hersh was a tough guy," Sands said. "He knew what he wanted, and he went all-out to get it. Sure, that rubbed some people up the wrong way. But we don't work with criminals. SHS's clients are good people who've been unjustly wronged. Yes, all of them, we're very proud of that. Recently, he'd been working on landing an account with Midhurst, the developers. He just pipped Clifton Smith of Eagletons to the post. But Cliff committing murders just because he lost a big account? Eagletons' have been struggling, but I *really* don't think so.

He's not that angry. Surely."

Josh caught the victim's assistant, Mamie Woods, at her usual lunch-time coffee shop, and introduced himself by offering condolences on her loss. "Oh, thank you, Mr. . . . ? Oh, hello Mr. Cole. No, I don't remember him mentioning you. It was first thing this morning, yes. When I got there, the police had arrived. Um, no, he was killed outside his home. Well yes, it's incredibly horrible, and I'd have rather gone home, but they need me to sort through some documents. How did you say you knew him?"

Eagletons had offices not far from SHS, and Clifton Smith was happy to answer a few questions about Hershel Swaggerty. "The man's a snake," Smith said. "He's got the morals of a jellyfish. Oh, there's nothing anyone could prove, but you hear the gossip, don't you? I wouldn't be surprised if I heard that he was out dining with a Mob boss, or helping a crooked politician cover up some huge fraud. What? *Murdered*? Oh, no. That's horrific. What a terrible loss. The city is much poorer for it. We've lost a great lawyer today. A great lawyer. Please leave me."

Back at the newsroom, Josh had several notes from his contact at the police station asking him to call. He got on the telephone immediately.

"Hey Josh," Pete said. "We're announcing the Swaggerty murder at nine tomorrow. The boys found another vic after I spoke to you last time. He's low-profile, some delivery guy who they reckon was just an unlucky bystander. Name was Dave Carey from a company called Roberts and Son. Mid twenties, but I don't have anything else on him."

"That's OK," Josh said. "A second vic adds splash, but the details won't matter as much. Anything else on Swaggerty?

"Some. We've tied him to the Italians—nothing that we could have made an arrest over, but enough to be damned certain he was on their team. He also forked over a large sum to someone undocumented recently. Looks like he was after some information."

"Leverage on Midhurst?"

Pete paused. "The developers? Huh. Could be, yeah. Did they work on a marina in the last couple of years?"

"Maybe. Look, I gotta go. I owe you."

"Yeah, you really do."

"Thanks, Pete. There'll be a not-so-little something extra for you this week."

Joshua hung up, and leaned back thoughtfully. Then he realized that he knew who the killer was.

Who does Joshua suspect, and why?

HINTS

STATEMENT

A Nascent Scandal

Vida Teague was an up-and-coming actress—petite, lovely, and a mercurial ball of nerves. A weary-looking sergeant escorted her into Inspector Parnacki's office, and she no sooner stepped through the door than she burst into tears. The sergeant introduced her, and fled.

"I'm so sorry, Inspector," she said, once the tears subsided. "You must think I'm a goose. It's just such a relief to know that *the* Paddington Parnacki is going to save my very life!" Her voice throbbed with uncertain emotions.

He permitted himself a soothing smile. "How may I assist, Miss Teague?"

"I . . ." She trailed off. Then she rallied, and when she resumed, she sounded far more matter of fact. "I've been bloody stupid. I let my man badger me into having a nasty little photographer snap some compromising images. Bird, his name is. Ellsworth Bird. The photographer, I mean. I've got a part in the new Chambers play, *The King In Yellow*, and I'll be touring for a few months. John begged for something to keep me in his thoughts, and insisted Bird was reliable and discreet. I'm afraid I was a little tipsy. We went to Bird's studio, so John could ensure that we got both the plates and the negatives right then. That was three nights ago."

"I begin to understand," Parnacki said.

"Quite. The robbery was last night. I got home from work

slightly early. I distinctly heard a drawer close, so I called out, but there was no answer. I grabbed a poker from the fireplace and very nervously made my way upstairs. I found my bedroom turned over, the negatives gone, and the window gaping wide. I made sure they were missing, of course. Even checked the wardrobe tops frantically. Just in case."

"Naturally," he murmured.

"Then I stumbled downstairs with an armful of blankets, and cried myself to sleep. Spending the night up there felt like a violation. I was still on the couch when an envelope arrived with the prints, and a note demanding a substantial sum of money. My father *could* pay it, but he's already mortified by my becoming an actress. I'd have to agree to enter a convent or something. But if the images are released, my career will be over. I really am in a serious bind."

Parnacki nodded thoughtfully. "I assume no one knows about the images, apart from John and the photographer?"

She sighed. "Bird had company. A girl I know vaguely from the circuit, a silly little thing with huge eyes, named Corinne Cooper."

"So three, then," Parnacki said. "You have the note?"

She passed it over. He studied it carefully. It was just a number, neatly typed. Substantial, indeed—it would have taken him a decade to earn that amount. He filed it as evidence, and started taking a statement.

Some two hours later, Teague was showing the inspector into her rooms on the lower two floors of an attractive building in the heart of the city. The front door had clearly been jimmied, but there was little evidence of intruders inside.

"It's just the bedroom that was ransacked," she told him, voice cracking a little. "I searched of course, but it's mostly as they left it." She took him up to the room, then went back downstairs, sniffling quietly.

Teague's bedroom was large, generously furnished, and in

considerable disarray. The window was still open, and October had settled in with a vengeance. The light was on, and the large ceiling fan was running, adding to the cold draught. The street below was surprisingly loud. Inspector Parnacki refastened his coat tightly. There were two tall wardrobes, both of them open and untidy. The cupboard was emptied, and even the dresser's little drawers had been removed and dumped on the floor. Clothing, make-up, and other personal effects had been carelessly scattered all over the floor.

Treading carefully, he went over to the window. There were no signs of damage or forcing on the woodwork. He poked his head out. Directly below, some 15 feet down, was a bare flower-bed with a deep pair of bootmarks driven into the soil. The toes of the boots were facing the wall.

He turned back round to let his gaze wander around the devastated bedroom. "All seems clear enough," he murmured.

What has Parnacki noticed?

HINTS
OCTOBER

The Missing Earrings

Miss Miller had known Bonnie Keeler for more than a decade. Keen ornithologists, the pair made a point of going into the countryside together every month or so, except during the colder parts of winter. They did not often visit each other's homes, however, and Miss Miller was interested when she got the chance to look around her friend's sitting room one chilly afternoon.

The focus of the room was a pair of comfortable couches in an elegant shade of blue, framing a glass and wicker coffee table. A pair of geraniums on the windowsill bracketed a vibrantly hued hibiscus, which strained away from the sunlight to face into the room. The walls were decorated with attractive pastoral paintings, and some exquisite drawings of birds of paradise. In the corner, a glass case contained a wide

selection of avian figurines in a range of styles.

"This fellow is spectacular," Miss Miller said, gesturing to a particularly lovely illustration of a raggiana.

"Thank you," Bonnie said. "I found him at a rather nice little auction a couple of years ago. I don't think you've seen him before. I didn't invite you over just to talk about birds, though."

Miss Miller arched an eyebrow. "Oh?"

"No," she said, darkly. "It's Rosalia."

"Ah." Rosalia Bohanan, Bonnie's niece, was a troubled young woman. She'd lost her mother at the age of two, and her childhood had not been easy. Recently, she'd started going off the rails in ways that worried her aunt.

Bonnie pinched the bridge of her nose, and sighed. "She's lifted little things before, but I let it slip. This time, it's my diamond earrings. They were in here—and then Rosalia was and the earrings were not, if you see what I mean."

"Yes, I'm rather afraid I do," said Miss Miller.

"I found her in here and came in, and she gave me one of those challenging looks she's so good at. I'd left the earrings on the table before lunch, and they were conspicuously absent. She noticed that I'd spotted them, and immediately got all defensive about it. Before I even said anything, mind."

"That's reasonably clear."

"Well, it's my fault really. I shouldn't have left them out, not with her around for lunch. I do know better. She's a darned magpie. Other things I've written off, or quietly had her father retrieve from her stashes a few weeks later, but my earrings are quite valuable, and I wouldn't put it past the girl to swap them for a couple of quarts of gin, or something equally idiotic. I really do feel sorry for her, and I'm very glad that I didn't have to go through the things she's gone through, but I also do want my earrings back."

"Did you try talking to her?"

"Of course. But you know what angry young women are like. She reacted badly, pretending to be deeply offended. Then she turned her pockets inside-out and insisted that I search her. After I refused, she flounced out. Then she was back yesterday, all sunshine and flowers, pretending nothing had ever happened. I didn't leave her alone for a moment, though. I'm sure she was up to something further."

Miss Miller looked around the room thoughtfully. "She probably hid them in here somewhere, if she wanted to be searched, and was then back pretending to be carefree. Did you come in here yesterday?"

"No, actually."

"In that case," Miss Miller said, "I suspect I know exactly where your earrings are."

Where are the earrings?

HINT
SUNLIGHT

The Late Mr. Early

Charlton Down Farm was on the edge of the city's official borders. Nestled on the hills it took its name from, it had a distinctly rural feel. Standing in the central courtyard, Inspector Parnacki could hear birdsong rather than cars, and the immediate horizon was dominated by trees rather than towers. It was a refreshing change. The manager of the Farm, Addison Early, had been bludgeoned to death after lunch, which finished at 12.30, and before 2pm, when his body was discovered. The crime scene yielded no immediately important information.

Most of the staff were still out around the farm doing their various tasks, so the inspector decided to start by talking to the farm's cook, Annabelle Burkhart. Mrs. Burkhart was in her forties, with the sort of stocky build that often hid surprising strength.

"What can you tell me of Mr. Early?" Parnacki asked her.

"I won't speak ill of the dead," said Mrs. Burkhart flatly. "He was a ruddy idiot, with bad language to make a sailor blush. Nothing went wrong that he didn't blame on one of the lads, and start screaming about. Anything that went right was his personal due, and should have gone better. Farm'll run a darn sight more efficiently with him out of the picture."

"I appreciate your restraint," he said. "Forgive my asking, but what were your movements after lunch?"

She squinted at him suspiciously. "After the washing up, I

went out to the dairy shed and continued working on the cheese. When I finished that, I went to ask his nibs if he wanted me to start on the hams, and found him with his head stove in. So I reported that to the police, grabbed myself a gin, and waited for you to arrive. And here you are."

"I see. Who else is here today?"

"Theo, Clay, and Emory. They'll be coming in for their cup of tea soon. You can talk to them then. Early's wife ran off last year, she's up north a way nowadays. Afore you ask, no, not unless she

crept back here like a mouse. Dairy barn is that one there, by the gate. Cheesing's not loud. I'd have heard a vehicle arrive."

A few minutes later, the farm hands started trickling into the courtyard. First back was Theo Shultz, the tractor-man, whose approach in an impressively modern Iver tractor seemed deafening after the relative quiet. A tall man with thinning hair, he wore heavy blue dungarees over a plain gingham shirt, both items liberally smeared with thick black grease. He took the news of Early's death impassively. "I been ploughing stubble back in all day, sir," he said. "Came back for lunch, went out again, back to the old croft. Witnesses? A whole bunch of magpies saw me out there, if that helps." Then he cackled.

Clay Crowson looked to be a similar age to Shultz, in his late thirties. He was wearing a rumpled white linen shirt and a pair of heavy denim trousers. Both were splotched with drops of green paint, but otherwise reasonably clean. When the inspector told him that Early was dead, he grinned for a moment, before forcing a more respectful expression onto his face. "I've been in the southern barn all afternoon, moving bales of hay around to make room for the next load. Thirsty work. I wouldn't say that I got on particularly well with Mr. Early, no, but then I wouldn't say that anyone got on particularly well with Mr. Early. Even his cats hated him. Whoever the firm puts in next, they'd be hard pressed to be worse."

The last worker, Emory McCammon, was a younger, thickset man wearing a dirty smock, heavy trousers, and filthy rubber boots. Parnacki explained that the manager was dead. "Right y'are, sir," McCammon said. He looked slightly confused. "Lookin' after the cows," he managed, when the inspector asked about his whereabouts at the time of the murder. The odour coming off his boots certainly seemed to suggest veracity. His response to the issue of whether he'd gotten on well with Mr. Early was even more laconic: "Nope."

Having waved McCammon onwards, Parnacki strolled around the courtyard a couple of times, thinking. Then he made his way to the kitchen, where the four had congregated. Conversation ceased, and they all turned to face him. "One of you is a liar," he said, "and, I strongly suspect, a murderer. It will be much better for you if you come clean right now. This is your only warning."

Who is lying?

HINTS
JOBS

The Ice Room Murder

The *Chronicle's* Howard Phillips, their hardest-hitting investigative reporter, was found dead on Monday morning. As his opposite number at the *Sentinel*, Joshua Cole was simultaneously saddened, unnerved and intrigued by his colleague's death. It was a general rule in the criminal underground that one didn't kill newspaper men unless it was absolutely necessary. Josh was digging into the story even before his editor gave him the assignment.

His first call was to his contact in the police department. "Hey Pete, it's Josh."

"Let me guess. Phillips."

"Yeah."

Pete sighed. "It's obviously the Mob. He was killed in a fish cannery officially owned by Benny Lucas's three-year-old niece. The place is a dilapidated piece of trash, even by the uniquely low standards of dockside warehouses. They shot him, chest and head, and left him in the ice room, so we've got no idea when he died. Some time after Thursday afternoon, when it closed for the long weekend, and before Monday morning, when it reopened. Friends say he'd often vanish for days at a time when he was onto something. No one had spoken to him in person for about a week. Without a time of death, we can't even begin to put a proper investigation together."

"Which explains why you're being so forthcoming today,

huh?" Josh said.

"Yeah, well, if you dig up anything, be sure to share. We'll find the flophouse he must have been staying at sooner or later, but the longer it takes to sort out his movements, the harder this'll be to nail."

Phillips's colleagues at the *Chronicle* were also unusually forthcoming. Clearly a murder in the family was just the thing for setting rivalries aside. Verne Handley covered City Hall and major sports. It was a peach of a gig, and he knew it. "Poor Howard," he said. "I knew this would happen sooner or later. He was an absolute bulldog. Once he had a story between his teeth, there was nothing that could make him drop it. He believed in the truth like it was a holy writ, no matter who it might hurt. He'd been excited for a couple of weeks, but of course he wasn't talking about it. Never did, until he filed his copy. He wasn't easy to like, but I respected the hell out of him."

Domingo Crujias handled business and finance. He was a neat man who was usually armed with a well-practised warm smile. "Howard was a friend," he told Josh. "I mean, really. We went to games together. He was on to something that he thought would reshape the city. I begged him to drop it. Some of my sources were talking about rising tension, and I even started having dreams about it, weird ones. I'm not surprised that he was killed, but I am sad. I saw him last Sunday. Not yesterday, eight days ago. A few of us had a beer. He was full of hints, said he'd be dark for a week or two, then he'd break the town apart. Damn it."

The international news editor was Sam Moyes, a rangy guy in his twenties. "I feel dreadful about Howard. I was the one who set him on that hunt. If I'd had any idea . . . I got word from a guy I know in Caracas about an illict shipment, disguised as fish. Howard had asked me to let him know about any smuggling I caught wind of, so I passed it on. That was a week ago. Now he's dead. If I'd just kept my damned mouth shut—but I didn't, did I? So I lit a candle for him yesterday. He was a good man, and a fine journalist, with a rock-solid code of honour that reflected his belief in the importance of the truth. We need more men like that."

As soon as he got back to the newsroom at the *Sentinel*, Josh was on the phone to Pete down at the station. "You won't believe this," he told his friend.

"What is it?" Pete asked. "You know something about Phillips?"

"Not me—but I know a man who does."

Who does Josh suspect of involvement?

HINT

AWARENESS

The Overton House

Regina Irwin was concerned. "Something isn't right, Mary." She paused to pet Miss Miller's calico cat, Aubrey, who had leapt onto her lap and was rubbing his head against her arm in a reassuring manner.

"I admit that I don't know the Overtons as well as you do," Miss Miller said. "But moving house can be a very tedious business. Isn't it possible that Lucille was just caught up in getting things prepared?"

"No," Regina said, flatly. "Marvin said that she'd gone ahead to Saliston, taken the train in a dreadful rush to be sure of being there when the movers arrived with their furniture. Lucille never did anything in a dreadful rush in her entire life. Besides, we see each other at least once a day, sometimes twice. It's unthinkable that she wouldn't have said farewell."

"I suppose you've had a word with Marvin?"

"Of course. He insists everything is perfectly fine, and that I'm probably over-stressed because Lucille and I are being separated. Could you talk to him? If there's anything going on, I know you'll be able to ferret it out."

"I'd be delighted to," Miss Miller said, smiling to disguise an internal sigh.

The Overton house was a pleasant four-bedroom building with generous gardens, in one of the city's quieter, leafier areas. She rang the bell. Footsteps approached, and Marvin Overton opened the door, hammer held loosely in one hand. Behind him, the hall was completely bare of furniture or fittings.

"Mary Miller! What a lovely surprise."

"Hello, Marvin," she said. "I'm glad I caught you. I wanted to say goodbye before you upped anchor."

"You cut it close. I'm waiting for the new owners some time this afternoon. Once they've got the keys, I'm off. I would invite you in—"

"Very kind," Miss Miller said, and stepped past him into the hall. "It's always fascinating to see a house in its most basic state, don't you think? Like a lovely young woman without makeup." She gestured up the stairs, then wandered through into the former living room. It too was almost completely empty. Bare wooden floors, plain off-white walls, and empty light fixtures. The fireplace, with a small mirror hung off-centre above it, gave the eye something to settle on.

Marvin noticed her glance, and waved the hammer sheepishly. "Old smoke-stain. Thought I'd make it look a little better for the new arrivals."

"Good of you. Is Lucille around?" she asked lightly.

"Sadly, no. She went ahead last night. The train takes almost as long to get to Saliston as the furniture people do, and she wants to be there when everything arrives. You know how she is. Everything has to be just so!"

"Indeed I do. How has the move been?"

"Oh, about as hellish as could be expected. The dashed paperwork took forever. We got everything boxed and had decorators slap a quick coat of whitewash all round to tidy up the walls. That meant a couple of nights in the Grand. They somehow managed to ruin my globe in the process, even though it was well covered. Then the removal men went through the place like a plague of clumsy locusts of course. There's a desk

I'm quite concerned about, and I'm certain that they broke the champagne flutes. I'll be extremely glad when this is all done with."

"I'm sure you will," said Miss Miller. "Regina Irwin seemed quite put out that Lucille didn't get a chance to make her farewells. No doubt a letter will soothe her."

"Yes, poor Regina seemed quite distraught. She and Lucille are thick as thieves, of course. But what with all the chaos, some things had to give. She's quite jumpy sometimes, Regina, as I'm sure you've noticed."

"She can get a little carried away," Miss Miller said. "Well, I mustn't keep you, Marvin. Best of luck with your new home."

Regina was waiting in a small park a little way down the road. Miss Miller sat down next to her on the bench.

"Well?" Regina demanded.

"You're right," Miss Miller said. "He's lying through his teeth."

Why does Miss Miller say Marvin is lying?

HINT
ACTIVITY

Bullet to the Brain

As suicide notes went, Louie Rodgers's was comparatively unflinching. "I never wanted to be this scumbag I've become," it said. "I spend my days terrorizing wounded veterans and little old ladies out of money they need to spend on food, just to provide some super-rich bank with a safety net—a safety net they're denying to the people who actually need one. I understand now. It's not right. I can't do this any more. I can't be this person. It's better for the world if I'm not in it."

He certainly looked at peace, Inspector Parnacki thought—apart from the damage to the back of his head, of course. Rodgers's body was reclined back in his office chair, hands clasped together over his chest. The suicide note and the pistol he'd apparently killed himself with were beside him, on his desk. A neat stack of papers sat on one side of the desk, and a pair of complex-looking ledgers on the other. The only other item on it was a supposedly humorous desk block facing the door, which declared that something scatological "stops here".

Rodgers's secretary, Helene Duggan, was in the front room. She was in a bad state, her makeup stained with tears. She saw the inspector walk back into the room and fixed him with an owlish stare. "I found him," she said. "I found him. I found him."

"Miss Duggan," the inspector said, gently. She jumped slightly. "Can you tell me what happened today?"

"I went out to lunch," she said. "He needed another person for the first time, and I wasn't there. I called for Roberta, and we went out for a sandwich and a coffee."

"Roberta is Roberta Valentine, Bruce Stanton's secretary?"

"Yeah. We went out. Gerry saw us go. I had cheese and tomato. It wasn't very good. It never is, you know? But you live in hope. Roberta had egg salad. She enjoyed it, I think. She talked about Bruce, how much of a sleaze he is, how he only seems to get clients fighting violent charges. There always seems to be some nasty piece of work in there, giving her the eye while her boss does his level best to ensure the guy escapes the justice he deserves. It's disheartening, you know? But it's not much better here, with Lou. He's OK with me, but what he does is shake little people down for their scraps

of money. He's like the Mob, but somehow it's all legal. The ones I get in here are pathetic, broken, tragic people, desperate to find some way not to end up in the gutter. Lou was one of them once, before he clawed his way up a rung, so he don't got no sympathy. He's terrified of ending up back down there with them, so whatever it takes to squeeze some cash out of them, he'll do it."

She sighed raggedly, and the inspector seized his chance. "What about after lunch, Miss Duggan?"

"When we got back, Gerry was dozing. He usually is, lunchtimes. We came up quietly. He's a sloppy guard, but he's a nice guy. I could smell something as soon as I came inside the office. My mind froze, and I went into Lou's office on autopilot. There he was. God, he's dead, and it's my fault. I shoulda been here."

"On the contrary," Inspector Parnacki said. "If you'd been here, you'd probably have been murdered as well."

Why does Inspector Parnacki think it's murder?

HINT

CHEST

The Resplendent Petunia

Despite being an ornithologist rather than a horticulturalist, Miss Miller often found herself on the judges' panel at the yearly flower show. Every time, she attempted to convince the organizer, her friend Maisie, that she was utterly unsuitable. Most years, Maisie replied that Miss Miller had a keen eye for both hue and character. This year, she had gone so far as to declare herself utterly desperate for a fourth judge, so once again, Miss Miller had done her reluctant duty.

After the prizes had been awarded, Miss Miller headed straight for the refreshments area, and sat down with a more or less tolerable pot of tea, and a slice of Victoria sponge. She was just starting to relax when a tall, well-tanned fellow sat down at her table and introduced himself.

"I do apologize for my impertinence, Miss Miller," he declared, giving her a smile he clearly considered winning. "Casper Griffiths is my name. I was very impressed with your discernment during the contest. May I impose on you for a moment of your time?"

She considered brushing him off, but Maisie's hurt expression swam into her imagination. She sighed. "Very well, Mr. Griffiths. How may I be of assistance?"

"How much do you know about petunias?" he asked.

"They're the Solanaceae family, like chili peppers, tomatoes, potatoes, and tobacco. Reasonably hardy annuals. Come in a range of pinks and purples, primarily."

"Excellent! You know, I assume, that a natural, bright emerald petunia is something of a holy grail? Well, I have done the impossible. I have found the holy grail!"

"Oh?" she murmured.

"It only grows in a tiny patch of dangerous territory on the border between Brazil and Uruguay. This area is home to a tribe of violently aggressive cannibals, so it's very difficult to get to. I lost a guide and a colleague to the savages, good friends both, but I managed to escape with a collection of seeds. It's a prize worth ten times its weight in diamonds."

"Well, surely—" she began.

"Now, I'm no horticulturalist. I'm a direct sort of man, one of probity and action. The world of cultivation is strange to me. My friend, Ben, the one who knew about this stuff, well, he's buried on a wild Brazilian hillside. I want to fund a second expedition, better armed, to bring him back home. So I'm prepared to sell the seeds to someone like yourself—an honest, hard-working expert."

"I'm hardly an expert—"

"You're too modest," Griffiths said, interrupting her again.

"The value of these seeds is incalculable. Ben explained it all to me, how if you grew these seeds into flowers, each plant would be providing you with a reliable income stream for years. Decades, even. You would, quite literally, be the envy of every grower. Your initial investment would earn back a fortune. The head-hunters of that region consider the plant sacred, you see. The emerald flowers are said to be the green blood of their heathen snake-god. They chased us down from the mountains and into the jungle, following for days. It was only by the narrowest margin—and the skill of my craft—that I managed to escape intact. No other white man knows where to find these flowers, and I'm done with it. I just want Ben's bones back in a Christian graveyard, somewhere his wife and daughter can pay their last respects. I'm sure you understand."

"I do indeed," she said. "I want to help. Please wait here. I must go and collect my purse."

Leaving Griffiths at the table, Miss Miller went to find Maisie. Apologizing to the bishop her friend was with, she pulled her aside swiftly. "Maisie, do you know if there's a policeman here at the show? A security guard would do. Some dreadful idiot is attempting to defraud me."

How does she know for certain that Griffiths is a fraudster?

HINT
CLASSIFICATION

The Bloody Name

When Joshua Cole arrived at the building that housed the offices of Sweetwater Green, he discovered the *Chronicle's* Lawrence Addison just leaving. Addison shot him a nasty grin, and dashed to get to the taxi that Josh had just exited. Fighting the urge to grind his teeth together, Josh made his way into the building. The harried-looking desk clerk issued him a visitor badge without even asking. Between police and press, it was likely a crazy afternoon.

Up on the fourth floor, the firm's rooms were in considerable disarray. Josh turned his visitor's badge the wrong way round and slipped into the suite while no one was looking. The statement that had been released so far was that Sweetwater Green honcho Burl Tuck had been found murdered in his own office. His partner, Lucius Ray, had issued a brief statement describing the death as shocking and horrifying. Gossip added that Tuck had written a name on the wall in blood.

A seemingly shell-shocked young man was sitting on a sofa in the reception area, clutching a notepad. Josh walked over, and sat down beside him, smiling.

"How are you doing?" he asked.

The guy looked at him. "I don't know. Everything is wrong. Who are you?"

"A friend. My name is Josh."

"Oh. Can you help it make sense, Josh?"

"Of course. Talk me through it once more, and we'll sort it all out."

"You can help?"

"Yes."

The man sighed. "Okay. The morning was quiet. There was a lot of paperwork. Mr. Tuck had a 9am with Mr. Ray. They didn't

seem happy, but Mr. Tuck assured me it was all okay, Mr. Ray was just having a few problems. Then we worked on some case paperwork for a while." His eyes glazed over, and he fell silent for a long moment.

Josh patted his shoulder sympathetically.

He came back to himself. "A new client came in at twelve. Mr. Ray was busy, so Mr. Tuck told me to show him in. I got his information and took him into the office, and then I went to start some filing. I think they started discussing Mr. Ray. I finished the filing after lunch, and discovered that Mr. Winter from First Agricultural was waiting in the conference room. Mr. Tuck hates being late, so I went in to remind him. He was slumped against the wall, white and cold. He wasn't moving. There was . . . blood. Lots of it. And the name, beside him. His fingertip was still red." He trailed off.

"So he did write it, then."

"Why would he do that? Why would he write his own name? I know who he is. Did he think I'd forget?"

"I'm sure it's not that," Josh said, as soothingly as he could. "What happened next?"

"I screamed for help, of course. What else could I do?"

"It was the right thing to do." Josh peered at the guy's staff badge. "Uh, Jan."

"Then the police came. All they do is ask questions. I still don't understand. You said you'd help."

"Well, I think . . . I think it was like his signature, on his life. Like he was signing the end of a document. He must have done that a lot, right?"

"Sure."

"So there you are. It was his signature. Him signing off."

"That . . . that makes sense," Jan said, doubtfully.

"See, I said I'd help," Josh said. "Could I have a look at your notepad?"

"I suppose." He handed it over.

Josh scanned the front page. It was secretarial notes for the day. "You've showed this to the police, I assume?"

Jan looked round at him. "You aren't with the police?"

"Well," Josh said quickly, "I'm not one of the detectives."

"Oh, I see. Yes, I've shown it to them."

"Great." He ripped the front page off, and handed the pad back to the surprised young man. "Thank you." There was a phone sitting on the front desk, opposite the sofas. He darted over to it, and called his editor. "There was a name on the wall by Tuck's body, chief," he told him. "His own. I know why, and it sure as heck wasn't a signature."

What does Josh mean?

HINT

IDENTITY

ire in the House

Inspector Parnacki stood in the roofless ruins of the burned house. It had been a compact but attractive property the day before. Now it was just so much rubble waiting to be torn down. There was no question of attempting to save the remains. A large, ugly vase had somehow survived without breaking—although the glaze had crazed nastily—and a patch of garishly cheerful living room carpet in the shape of a prone woman clearly showed where the fire's victim, Jewel Francis, had been removed from. Otherwise, everything was black and charred.

The victim's husband, Tom Francis, had suffered minor smoke inhalation and spent the night in hospital. He'd painted a bleak picture. "I can't believe that she's gone. It was so stupid, and so like her. I woke up coughing and smelled smoke. It must have been one in the morning. Jewel was still asleep, but I hauled her out of bed, and hurried the two of us downstairs. The

kitchen and living room were already blazing, but we were able to dash through the hall fairly safely. I thought we'd escaped. Then we remembered Dottie, our cat. Jewel shrieked, and then she was running back in. I tried to stop her, but she was too fast. I screamed for her to come back. Then the door collapsed. I did, too. I don't remember much else."

Exiting the burnt-out home, the inspector saw the resident of the house next door and went over to speak to him. "Mr. McCulley?"

"That's right," the man said.

"My name is Inspector Parnacki. I understand you found Mr. Francis and contacted the fire brigade."

"That's right. I don't sleep so well any more. I saw the flickering light, so I got up and looked outside. Tom's house was burning down. I called the fire service and then went out to see if I could help. Tom was on the pavement, covered in soot. He looked stunned. When I asked about his wife, he just shook his head. When the firemen came, I told them that I thought a woman was in there, but there wasn't anything they could do by then. They pulled Tom back, away from the house, and did what they could. Stopped it spreading, at least. There was quite a crowd by then. I saw ambulance people take Tom off, which was a mercy. His breathing didn't sound so great."

"Do you know if the couple had any pets?"

"A cat, I believe. I'd see her out in the garden, from time to time. I'll keep an eye out for her."

Apart from her husband, the last person to have seen Jewel

Francis alive was a friend, Lulu Kirke. She lived just a few blocks away, so Parnacki strolled to her home. When she answered the door, it was obvious that she'd been crying. The inspector introduced himself, and followed her through into her kitchen.

"Jewel was good, Inspector. She was happy. She and Tom were getting on well, like always. Maybe he worked a bit too hard, but then most men do in my experience. We talked about making jam, and about going up to the shops next week, and she and Tom coming round to us for dinner. How can she be dead, and the sun just shining on like that, as if nothing's happened?"

"What can you tell me about Mr. Francis?"

"Tom? He's a decent man, polite, well-behaved. Drinks wine. Gets a bit grumpy when he's tired. Likes tinkering with machinery in his shed. Lord, I don't know. He's normal. He's seemed a bit more smiley the last couple of months, but he's never been the unhappy type."

"Thank you for your time," the inspector said.

When he got back to the station, he called Officer Sullivan in. "The Francis fire is almost certainly murder, not misadventure," he said.

Why does Inspector Parnacki suspect murder?

HINT
BURNS

Death at the Table

Katherine Mayes had been sitting in the kitchen with a mug of coffee and a romantic novel. Her killer had apparently come in through the back door and strangled her. Inspector Parnacki had taken a quick look at the body before it was removed and hadn't seen any obvious signs of other assault or struggle. The back door opened on to a small, tidy garden, at the rear of which was a gate to the alley beyond. The back fence hid most of the alley, but from what the inspector could make out, it looked quietly neglected. If there were signs of passage back there, Officer Sullivan would find them.

The dead woman's husband, Eli Mayes, was now slumped at the kitchen table. He wore an off-white sweater and dust-streaked tan slacks, and had been on the floor next to his wife right up until the technicians had shooed him away. He was staring off into nowhere miserably.

Parnacki pulled out a chair and sat down at the table with him. "Why don't you talk me through the day's events, Mr. Mayes?"

He glanced up from his hands. "What? Oh. Yes, of course. We got up at eight-thirty, as usual for Sundays, and had some breakfast before church. It was a little after ten when we got back. Kate has been on at me to repaint the front porch, so I collected my stuff from the shed, mixed up a batch of royal blue undercoat and got to it. I was just about half-way done with the undercoat when I decided I really needed a drink, and came in here to get something."

The inspector nodded. The railing on the front porch had been tacky.

"That's when I found Kate. It must have been midday, I suppose. The back door was open, like it is now, and so was the garden gate. Why wouldn't they be? I managed to call for help, then I sat down with Kate. Is the kitchen clock right? Has it really been four hours? Anyway, I just sat there on the floor. With her. It didn't seem right to leave her alone. Now they've taken her away, and nothing makes a lick of sense."

"I'm very sorry for your loss," Parnacki said. "Did you see any sign of anyone while you were on the porch?"

"No, nobody. Sundays are quiet around here. Everyone's at church, or with family, or just away for the day. Elton and Selma Terry from three doors down are often about, but not today.

Thinking about it, I did hear a thump from back in the alley at one point, while I was painting, but I figured it was just a cat fooling around."

"Do you have any idea as to when it happened?"

"Just between ten-fifteen and midday, more or less. After I'd been with Kate for twenty minutes, I'm afraid I finished off her coffee. It was a running joke between us, that she'd never finish a hot drink. The coffee was slightly warm. That was the only moment that I left her side."

"I understand," Inspector Parnacki said. "Much as I hate to inconvenience you, Mr. Mayes, I'm going to have to ask that you come with me down to the station, where we can continue our conversation."

"I don't understand," Mayes said. "Am I under arrest?"

"If necessary. Do I need to arrest you for your wife's murder, Mr. Mayes?"

Why does Inspector Parnacki suspect Eli Mayes?

HINT

MOVEMENTS

Stanley's Narrow Escape

Annabel Voss was clearly still in shock. When her butler, Henderson, showed Miss Miller to her drawing room she got up, smiled, and invited her in, then called Henderson by his predecessor's name and burst into tears.

Miss Miller comforted her friend, while Henderson quietly went to fetch a pot of hot tea.

"It's unimaginable," Annabel said. "Some foul beast actually creeping in here and trying to kidnap Stanley away! It just doesn't ... This sort of thing doesn't happen. I ..." She trailed off, whimpering.

"How is he?"

"He's fine, of course. You know how seven-year-olds are. Everything seems to bounce straight off. I'm the one who's turned into a nervous wreck. It was Jettie and Selma who saved him."

"What exactly happened, Annabel?"

"Stanley was upstairs, playing with Selma. Gustav is on a business trip, but he's cutting it short. He'll be back this afternoon. I was in here, taking advantage of a very rare moment of silence to do some sketching. The peace was broken by the most god-awful shrieks suddenly, and several loud crashes, followed by quick, thudding footsteps. I dashed up the stairs a few paces in front of Henderson, and found Selma and Jettie crying and hugging Stanley. Some masked thug had burst in and tried to grab him. Jettie had begun screaming, while Selma pelted the intruder with anything that came to hand—an urn, some decorative plates, an ashtray, that sort of thing. Then she found a poker and actually went for him, and he fled. He jumped out of a hall window into the rhododendrons and ran off. The police took his description, and helped us find a reliable firm, so we have a very capable-looking man with Stanley and Selma now, but they don't think the kidnappers will try again."

"Horrible," Miss Miller said. The tea had arrived by that point, and she took a deep swig. "How did this fellow get in? I assume he didn't just waltz through the front door."

"Well, no, quite. The police didn't find any signs of a forced entry. Henderson would have had to let him in the front, and I'd have heard the door anyway. That leaves the kitchen door, the terrace door, or the French windows at the back. But Mrs. James was in the kitchen all afternoon, and Arlene was cleaning in the ballroom, which is where the terrace leads to. So they think it must have been the French windows. Maybe he had some way to unlatch them."

Miss Miller frowned. "Perhaps we should just have a little look."

"If you think it might help," Annabel said doubtfully.

Nodding, Miss Miller led her friend outside. The terrace was clear of furniture, the stone sparkling lightly in the morning sun. The large folding doors to the ballroom were closed. Annabel produced a small silver key and unlocked them. Miss Miller tugged on one, and it slid smoothly open.

"I suppose I'll have to get used to keeping these closed," Annabel said. "We rather rely on the terrace doors for ventilation in the summer."

"Shame," Miss Miller said.

The kitchen door was sturdy and functional rather than attractive. Cobwebs covered its upper reaches. Annabel knocked on it, and after the loud, heavy clunking of a key turning and a bolt shooting back, the cook pulled the door open, rendering a number of spiders suddenly homeless. "Ma'ams?" she said, looking suspiciously from Annabel to Miss Miller and back.

Miss Miller smiled at her. "Do you typically keep this door

closed, Mrs. James?"

The cook snorted. "Of course, Ma'am. Don't want no young rascals sneaking into the pantry and making off with my cakes."

Annabel smiled. "It only happened twice, as I recall."

"That's as before I started locking and bolting this door, Ma'am." A hint of a smile flickered over the cook's studiously ferocious face. "Need to get up early to put one over on Celeste James, so you do."

"Sorry to have disturbed you," Miss Miller said.

"Ma'am," said the cook, nodding regally. The door closed again, and was loudly resealed.

The French windows at the back of the house opened out from the long hall, providing access to the gardens. They were sealed tight, with a keyhole on the outside, but no handles. Miss Miller peered at the metal keyhole plate, but there was no sign of scratching or other damage. She stood back up, and was looking at the doors thoughtfully when Henderson walked past inside. A quick knock on the doors and a gesture sent him off to get the key, and a moment later he was back. He unlocked the French windows, and pushed them open with a piercing squeal of tortured wood.

"My deepest apologies," he said. "The frames warp in the spring, and the doors get a bit screechy. Mr. Voss and I have discussed shaving the bottom of the doors, but he feels that a winter draught would be the greater evil. I have taken the liberty of refreshing your teas."

Annabel thanked him, and the ladies re-entered the house. As they made their way back to the drawing room, Miss Miller glanced around to make sure they were alone, and said, "We need to speak to the police, Annabel. I think your kidnapper had someone on the inside."

Who does Miss Miller suspect, and why?

HINT
DOORS

The Gunman

Working evenings in a liquor store is one of the less safe options in the retail profession. According to the initial report that Inspector Parnacki had received, gunshots put the time of Tom Pearse's death at 7:18pm, according to witnesses in adjacent stores. By the time help had arrived, Pearse was dead, and his killer had vanished with the contents of the cash register.

The store had a run-down air about it. Shelves and finishings were aged, paint cracking in places. The various cabinets didn't match, and had been slapped into place haphazardly, covering the side door while leaving chunks of dead space in corners. The wooden floor needed entire beams replacing, and even the sound areas were wine-stained. The whole place screamed "good enough."

Pearse's body had been found behind the store's ratty counter. The empty register drawer stuck out above him. He'd been shot in the chest twice, neither shot hitting the heart. It suggested an amateur assassin, in keeping with the sort of violence that liquor stores typically attracted. The killer had left no overt evidence behind, so Parnacki left the store to the lab technicians and went to talk to the witnesses.

Daniel Whiddon had been the first to raise the alarm. He worked next door, in a grocery. He was 24, a gangly young man with a slightly nervous air about him. "I knew Tom to say hello to," he told the inspector. "He was older than me—thirty-five, I think—and wasn't particularly friendly. He was quite bitter, deep down. But we all have the same landlord on this side of the street, so we'd occasionally share complaints about the old skinflint. What? Oh. His name is Harry Hawke. Please don't say I called him a skinflint, he'd price me out completely. Right, last night. I heard gunshots from next door. Well, I assumed it was the liquor store. Who sticks up a sandwich guy? Anyway, I called the police, locked up, and went over there. Bill from the bar opposite was on his way over the road. Pete from the deli was in the store. He looked pale. Tom was already dead. I didn't see anyone on the street, no. He must have run off while I was getting help. The police were there within minutes."

Peter Davey, 29, worked in the delicatessen on the other side of the liquor store. "I didn't get a good look, but I did see the guy. I heard the shots and dashed out. I saw a tall, burly guy opening the door. He looked dumb and craggy, from the glimpse I got, and his nose was squashed, like a boxer's. I didn't want him seeing me, you know? So I ducked down the alley and went into the shop through the side door. Tom was behind the counter in a pool of blood. He was already dead, I think. A few moments later, Dan from the grocery rushed in, followed by Bill from the bar. The police weren't far behind. But there was nothing any of us could do. I wasn't close to Tom, no. He wasn't the kind of guy you get close to. But he didn't deserve to die like that, gunned down for the contents of his register."

William Brewer owned and ran The Brewery, the bar opposite the liquor store. He was a heavyset guy in his early fifties. "I heard the shots, sure. Came out, and saw Dan locking his place. I might have caught a glimpse of a tall guy walking away briskly, but it was dark, and it might have been my eyes playing tricks. When I got across the road, Tom was dead. There wasn't anything I could do, and you don't leave a bar with drinkers in it unattended, so I came back here. I lost a couple of bottles of hooch in the time I was gone, but it was only cheap stuff. I knew Tom, sure. He'd come in here after he closed up. He fit right in with the other patrons. This ain't a great part of town, you know? He didn't much like how life had turned out, but heck, down here, who does? Enemies? No, men like Tom are too self-absorbed to make enemies. People who don't give a damn about you don't become enemies. If he had any friends, I never met 'em. Wish I could tell you more. This sort of stuff is real bad for business. Anyway, more to the point, Tom might not have been a ray of sunshine, but he was a decent customer, and he could talk a good ball game."

After he'd left The Brewery, Inspector Parnacki looked across the road at the liquor store and the shops either side. "No need to go looking any further afield," he said thoughtfully.

Who does Parnacki suspect and why?

HINT
LOGISTICS

The Investigation

Murdered private investigators didn't usually make headlines, but Forrest Lewis had been digging into the affairs of mayoral candidate Nigel Pattison. That gave his death the vital whiff of scandal that the press liked. The leaked photo of the crime scene, complete with its mystery pearl-handled revolver dominating the dead man's desk, had been on all the front pages. Somehow, the *Tribune*'s David Southwell had managed to get details on the investigation—accusations of major fraud—and was raising reasonable concerns. The *Chronicle*'s Verne Handley was responding by tirelessly painting Pattison as a pure-bred saint. Josh, meanwhile, was in the doghouse again.

Pete, Josh's police contact, was discouraging. "Pattison's got clean hands," he said. "We already dug into him. Sure, he's most likely guilty, but there's never going to be a way to prove it. That's why his opponents went private—because we had to give up. Lewis was on a well-paid fool's errand. No way Pattison was in enough danger to risk having him killed. To make things worse, word from the lab is he wasn't even shot. That fancy gun you've all been talking up isn't the murder weapon. No, I don't know how he really died, they're keeping that under wraps for now. Sorry Josh, I know that's not what Marley wants to hear."

Thinking about his editor's wrath, Josh decided to set about talking to people from Lewis's personal life in the hopes of finding something that the *Chronicle* and *Tribune* might have missed.

Lewis's assistant, Rodney Cash, was a tough-looking but pleasant man in his early twenties. "I don't know what I can tell you, Mr. Cole," he said. "Enemies are a job hazard as a private investigator, but Forrest had been working on Pattison full-time for a month or more, so why now? People usually simmer down a bit with time, and Pattison seemed amused rather than upset or concerned. I don't know of anyone that Forrest put away recently getting out of prison. I was out, meeting a guy who claimed to have something we could use. Total waste of time, actually. He never showed. When I got back, they'd already taken the body away. The gun? No, Forrest would never have bought anything that showy. I assume the murderer ditched it."

Alfonso Parker was an old friend of Forrest's who'd met him for lunch earlier on the day of the murder. "We've known each other since school," he said. "He comes round to ours for dinner once every month or so, I guess. Came, I mean. Jeez. I'll miss the crazy schmuck. I was always scared this would happen one day, you know? Digging up dirt on politicians, that's far more dangerous than following cheating husbands. Lunch, yeah. We ate at April's, down from city hall. Forrest seemed a bit down, but he said his boy was out on a good lead. I think the case was getting to him. He said he hadn't made much progress, and that always ticked him off. Seems impossible that three hours later he'd have his head stove in. Just doesn't make sense. Lady friend? No, Forrest wasn't the relationship type. Poor devil."

Lewis's other employee—strictly part-time—was a former boxer named Vernal Leonards. Josh found him at the gym he ran. Leonards was in his early thirties, a mountain of muscle and scar tissue with a surprisingly gentle voice. "I heard about Mr. Lewis getting shot, sure. A real waste. He was a gent. Sure, I helped him out. When he needed a bit of protection. He was a smooth guy, not a fighter. Good-looking. I kept a few guys from him over the years, sure. Not many. People liked Mr. Lewis. Four years, I guess? Since I retired. I never met anyone who seemed to want to actually kill him. Threats, sure, now and again. But they were just words."

Leaving Leonards's gym, Josh made a beeline for the payphone outside, and dialled his editor's personal line. "Put me through to Reuben, Jenny. He's going to love this. I know who murdered the P.I."

Who does Josh suspect, and why?

HINT

AWARENESS

❧

The Golfer

Miss Miller pushed her calico cat, Aubrey, off her lap, and sat up a little straighter. "My dear Leta, you actually *found* her? I'm so sorry."

Leta Harvey nodded miserably. "I thought you knew. Yes, I'd arranged to drop round there to return a pair of binoculars I'd borrowed for the previous weekend. I could hear the kettle whistling, and the kitchen door was open, so I went on in. Faye was slumped over the table, dead as you like. I'm sure I shrieked for a while, and then I went to call the police." She paused. "There was obviously no point trying to help her. When I got back, the kettle had finally boiled dry. The constable said that probably meant that she'd been dead for ten or fifteen minutes when I arrived."

"I suppose so," Miss Miller said. "I assume you didn't see anything else odd or out of place?"

"No, nothing was disordered or out of place. The coffee and cream were out, and the icebox open, so I suppose he came in as she was putting the kettle on."

Miss Miller shook her head. "They've spoken to the husband, I presume?"

"Lonnie," Leta said. "Yes. They had him in for questioning that evening. He was golfing at the time. He'd signed in an hour earlier, and twenty upstanding citizens are happy to agree that he'd been in the bar of the 19th ever since he'd arrived. Lonnie Montgomery is a piece of work, no doubt about that, but it obviously wasn't him. At least, not in person."

"I don't know him. I might have met her once, at the Ornithological Society's annual bash."

"He's a smug, arrogant fool," Leta said. "I tried to time my visits and invitations to occasions when he wouldn't be available. I can imagine him flying into a rage, but not really having the gumption to hire someone to . . ." She trailed off, shuddering.

Mary Miller smiled sympathetically at the other woman. "I don't suppose that Faye was being . . . unwise?"

Leta laughed bitterly. "Faye? No. If it didn't have wings—or pages—she really wasn't that interested. Marion Woolley and I were probably her closest friends, and we were hardly her bosom buddies. I know that there's the cliché about quiet types having dark secrets, but Faye was just self-sufficient."

"Marion Woolley," said Miss Miller thoughtfully. "Now there's a woman with an interesting mind."

"Very much so. Sharp as a steel trap."

"She was a friend of Faye's as well?"

"Yes. I've known Marion for years of course, and Faye rather fell in with us. Generally, when I saw Faye, Marion was there too, and vice versa."

"Does she have any ideas?"

"She thinks that Lonnie is behind it somehow."

Miss Miller frowned. "You don't suppose that she . . ."

"Marion? Oh, she'd kill Faye off in a heartbeat in a novel, but in real life? No, absolutely not. The pen may be mightier than the sword, but I know which I'd rather have with me in a brawl."

"Leta, my dear, I do believe that's it."

"It is?"

"Yes! Well, no, not that precisely, but yes. I know how Lonnie Montgomery could have done it!"

Why does Miss Miller suspect Lonnie?

HINT

SET-UP

The Fabric Man

Isaiah Rule hadn't seen his attacker. He'd been in his stock room tallying supplies when he heard a footstep. The next thing he remembered was waking up several hours later, in hospital. Although he couldn't identify his assailant, with his assistance Inspector Parnacki been able to narrow the field to four primary suspects. These worthies were now awaiting interview.

Parnacki had barely taken his chair in the interview room when his assistant arrived with a mug of coffee.

"Thank you, John," Parnacki said.

"Did you hear about the gas main explosion on Randall Street yesterday afternoon, sir?"

"No. Injuries?"

"A few. Nothing serious. Caused havoc with the traffic right across the west side of the city, though."

Parnacki frowned. "Thank you. Was there anything else?"

"Hmm. More violence in Russia, a dancer embroiled with a fairly important politician, Petty missed the match with flu, nurses talking about walking out because of poor treatment. Oh, and unseasonal weather expected on Tuesday." He broke off, looking at the inspector's expression. "Ah. No. I'll bring in the first suspect, shall I?"

Inspector Parnacki nodded pleasantly. John paled, and scurried off to fetch the first interviewee.

Sherman Clinton was one of Rule's suppliers. Somewhere

under his mounds of wild hair, there appeared to be a well-muscled man in a suit. "I deal with Isaiah, yeah. I got suppliers out in the East—China, mostly—and they provide me with all sorts of stock. Lots of silk. Very popular, silk."

"Quite valuable, too," Inspector Parnacki observed. "I assume all your goods are fully accredited and show the proper customs payments?"

Clinton spread his hands wide, and grinned. "You're welcome to look at my books any time, Inspector. With the proper paperwork."

"Quite," Parnacki said. "Did you see Isaiah Rule yesterday afternoon?"

"No, of course not. I don't work on Saturdays. I was with my niece Adelina from 10am until 6pm, in fact. We went to the park. I was lucky to miss the traffic. My sister and her husband need a break from time to time, and I'm happy to oblige. Family is so important, don't you think?"

"I'm sure. Thank you for your time."

The next interviewee, Finley Koontz, was a regular at a coffee shop near Rule's warehouse. He'd been involved in a number of petty offences over the last year or two, but had yet to do anything worth prosecuting. He looked every bit as seedy as his history suggested.

"I know the guy you mean, yeah. Deals cloth. So what? I ain't no seamstress." Koontz snickered. "No, I ain't never been in there. Why would I?"

"Where were you yesterday afternoon, Mr. Koontz?"

"Where else? At the big game, along with every other guy worth talking about in the city."

"I didn't have the pleasure. Demands of the job."

"Ah, you missed a cracker. We thrashed them. I thought Parrott was supposed to be hot stuff, but he didn't even show. Wilkins folded like a cheap suit. Meanwhile, Carter and Petty were on fire. It was spectacular. They just melted away. There were some red faces up north last night, I'll bet."

Parnacki sighed. "Thank you, Mr. Koontz."

Carter Spurling was a former employee of Rule's. The two had parted ways acrimoniously, a few months previously. "Rule was a damned idiot," Spurling said. "I worked hard for him for five years. Of course I never stole anything from his petty cash. He was sure it was me, though. I was out the door before I could blink."

"Annoying," Inspector Parnacki said.

"I was furious." Spurling paused. "That don't mean I ripped him off, though. I didn't take his cash, and I didn't steal from his stock either. I don't do that stuff."

"Where were you yesterday afternoon, Mr. Spurling?"

"With my girl, Cee. Stuck on a bus all day, it felt like. When we got into the middle of town, we'd already missed her friends. She'll tell you all about it. She certainly told me all about it all darn night, and I was there. It's not my fault—and neither's Rule's misfortune, but he sure is welcome to it."

Tom Clabaugh, finally, was a minor career criminal with several convictions for assault and theft. He'd left a number of people unconscious in warehouses in the district over the last decade, many more than the police had been able to prove. He was a burly man a little shy of forty, with a habitually sullen expression.

"I don't know the guy you're talking about. I don't know his place. Maybe I been past, maybe not, but I never been in there. I was fishing down by the river all yesterday, sun up to sun down. Caught myself several big, fat trout. Ask around the boys down there, they'll tell ya. No, I don't know names. I was fishing, not making friends."

Parnacki thanked the man, and excused himself. Once outside the room, he called for his assistant. "Let's get started on the paperwork for an arrest, shall we?" he said.

Who does Parnacki suspect and why?

HINT

YESTERDAY

The Vinson Scandal

Annis Vinson was a familiar name to anyone with even a passing knowledge of the gossip columns. Old Meyer Vinson had made a fortune in copper back in the previous century, and a good quarter of the city had been built on his land. His children and grandchildren had settled comfortably into the role of local patricians, and the family's fortune and status had only swelled with time. The new generation of Vinsons seemed keen to do their best to deplete both, but age would mellow them into sense and respectability before much longer. For now, though, Annis and her siblings and cousins were a reliable source of column inches. Today, the news was that someone had burgled her apartment, and stolen a necklace, some rings, and a scandalous selection of lacy garments.

When a witness called the *Sentinel* saying he'd seen the burglar and offering to sell the scoop, Josh Cole had been unlucky enough to take the call. The society correspondent, Philip Carter, was off somewhere plush interviewing someone tedious about nothing much, as usual. The paper's editor was insistent that Josh had to go and speak to the witness immediately, and close a deal if possible. "He knows your voice, boy," Marley said. "You go. Now."

So Josh found himself uptown, the sole customer of a frighteningly expensive little coffee shop called *Le Cochonnet*, where the witness worked. After sighing over the menu, he ordered as plain a coffee as he could find, and a slice of something that looked like pie, and made a mental note to be darn certain to get the receipt. The waiter, Hayes Beauchamp, was the guy Josh was looking for. When the man fetched his order, Josh identified himself. Beauchamp nodded to his boss behind the counter, and dropped into the spare chair. His snooty French accent vanished.

"Pleasure to meet you, Mr. Cole."

"Yeah, me too," Josh said. "So you saw something yesterday?"

Beauchamp nodded. "It's explosive. So how does this work?"

Josh sighed. "We sign a non-disclosure, where you agree to tell me what you have and give us the right to purchase its exclusive use as a story if we want it, and we agree not to use a word of it until we've paid you." He named a figure about half as high as Marley had authorized him to go. "Then you tell me what you've got. If we're both happy, we sign a full agreement where we get full rights, you promise not to tell anyone else anything, and you get paid. Fair?"

"Yeah, sure."

Josh produced the NDA, and they signed.

Beauchamp smiled broadly. "You'll love this. So I'm in here all day, right. We're exclusive, so it's not exactly bustling. I was watching the street like usual when I saw this cop sidle up to Miss Vinson's door. Most cops walk purposeful, you know? This one, he looked . . . furtive. That's the word. He had his hat tipped down low, and dark glasses, and gloves too. I didn't think too much of it. It's not warm out there. But then he produces something from his pocket and fiddles with her lock, and a moment later, bam! He's in there, closing the door behind himself. Well, I was mighty curious then, so I watched the place. Five minutes later, he's back out again, just like before, but with a bulging satchel. He looks around from the doorway, then slips out onto the street, closing the door behind him. Then he's off, whistling on his merry way."

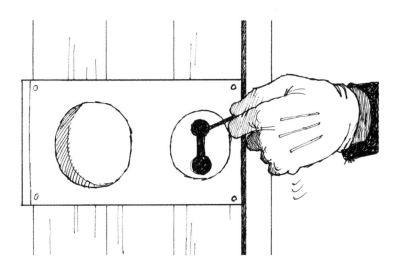

"That is quite something," Josh said. "Will you stand by that story? Did you get enough of a look for a description?"

"Of course I will," Beauchamp said. "But I don't want my name in the paper. Lou is happy to let me talk to you, but he said no mention of the shop."

"We can do that," Josh said.

"Great. The guy was about 6 foot 1 inch, broad nose, brown eyes, a square jaw with a wide mouth, and beefy-looking but not porky, you know? Like he knew his way around a fight. I could work with a sketch guy if you have one."

Josh finished scribbling notes. "Great. Let me check in with my boss, and I'll be back in two minutes." He left the café, and headed to the payphone on the street corner. He got through to his editor quickly. "Hey boss. I've spoken to the Vinson witness, and I don't believe a word of it. You want I should buy it?"

Why does Josh doubt the witness?

HINT
OBSERVATIONS

The Mugging

A brutal mugging on the way to the city's leading repairer of antique watches had left Jerry Lawrence hospitalized. His wallet, wedding ring, antique watch, and cufflinks had all been stolen, but fortunately, his brief spell of unconsciousness did not seem to have caused any obvious brain damage. Since the attack had taken place at around ten in the morning, Lawrence had been spotted swiftly by a member of the public. A quick police response had yielded several suspects who now, four hours later, awaited Inspector Parnacki's questions.

Elroy Syker was a thin, twitchy man with a long history of picking pockets. He looked up plaintively as Parnacki entered the room.

"Come on, Inspector. You know I ain't done nothing."

"You've told me that before, Mr. Syker," Parnacki said.

"Yeah, well, I mean it this time."

"What were you doing on Dell Street this morning?"

Syker shrugged. "Minding my own business." He sighed, and fished a handful of change out of his pocket. "Going to buy bread. See?"

"On Dell Street?"

"Course not. There's a little baker on Bradford Street that does lovely rolls."

"Have you ever seen this man before?" The inspector pushed over an image of Jerry Lawrence.

He shook his head. "Should I have?"

"Someone jumped him this morning. Was it you?"

Syker sneered. "Come off it, Paddington. I don't need to thump a guy to get his wallet off him, and you know it. He'd never even realize I'd been there—if I were to do such a thing. Which I never, ever would, obviously, it being illegal and all. So just cut me loose, would you? I missed breakfast, and now I've been here for hours."

The next suspect, Dana Steele, was big and muscular, and had spent some time in prison on robbery and smuggling charges a few years ago. He was sitting patiently in his chair when Parnacki went into the interview room, and didn't look up until the inspector sat down opposite him.

Parnacki introduced himself. "Why were you on Dell Street this morning, Mr. Steele?"

Steele shrugged. "Just out walking. It's easy to forget that there's a whole city out there sometimes. It's good to remind yourself." He looked at the picture that the inspector produced. "No, I don't remember that guy. If I've seen him before, he didn't make an impression. What does he do?"

"I believe Mr. Lawrence is an accountant, in fact. So you don't recall robbing him this morning?"

"I'll go one further, and say I definitely recall not robbing anyone this morning. I've learned my lessons, Inspector. I value the sky too much to engage in shenanigans of that sort any more. I hope you get your man, though."

The third suspect, Delbert Calfee, was pacing the room

irritably when Parnacki entered. He turned and glowered at the inspector, but took his seat again obediently enough for all that. Calfee was trim and bearded, with slicked-back hair. Like the other two, he had a criminal history, having been caught breaking and entering a couple of times in his early twenties.

"How much longer do I have to wait?" Calfee demanded. "I'm meeting my girl across town at one-thirty. I don't want to be late."

"Shouldn't be long now, Mr. Calfee," the inspector said. "Just a few questions. What were you doing on Dell Street this morning?"

"You held me here for hours to ask about my shopping habits? I was going to buy a new scarf, Inspector. Is that acceptable?"

"Quite prudent, I'd say. Did you happen to see this man while you were out?"

Calfee looked at the picture. "Nope. Never seen him before."

"So you didn't rob him this morning?"

The man rolled his eyes, and sighed. "No. I'm not in the habit of coshing random strangers and rolling them for their pocket change. I know I have a record, but I was a dumb kid, damn it. Not that your lot ever let me forget it."

Back outside the interview rooms, Parnacki shook his head wearily, and went to write up the arrest warrant.

Who does Inspector Parnacki suspect, and why?

HINT
KNOWLEDGE

The Clockwork Owl

Zelma Dalton was an avid collector of curios. She was particularly interested in automata, and the pride of her collection was a cat-sized pottery elephant from medieval India which, when wound, would flail its trunk around and rear up a little to stamp its feet. The city's annual collector's fair was one of the highlights of her year, and Miss Miller typically accompanied her, to look for interesting ornithological prints or sketches. They were joined this year by Rowena Elliott, a mutual friend who had an interest in miniatures of all descriptions.

Miss Miller was looking at some curiously unpleasant bas-reliefs of a rather amateurish cityscape when Zelma appeared at her shoulder. "What on earth is that, Mary? How horrid. I think I've found something interesting. Would you come and give me your opinion?"

"Of course," Miss Miller said.

Zelma led her through the fair to a smaller stand near the far wall. It was piled with a very random-seeming selection of items, ranging from obvious garbage to some quite nice pieces. In amongst them was a metal box about the size of Miss Miller's palm, and some five inches deep.

"May I?" Zelma asked the stand's attendant, a reedy-looking man with a thin moustache.

"Of course, madam," the man said.

Zelma opened the box. Inside was a dusty bronze owl, which blinked at them, turned its head to and fro, and emitted a small noise not unlike a hoot. The figure was well-designed, and quite life-like.

"Very impressive," Miss Miller said.

"Yes, it's quite fine," Zelma said. "Such things are not uncommon nowadays, but it's particularly interesting—and valuable—because of its age."

"Oh? How old is it?"

The attendant bobbed forward. "At least a century and a half, madam. My grandfather inherited it from his mother when she died. Apparently, it had been her greatest treasure, a gift from a suitor in her youth. She kept it in pristine condition on her mantle. My grandfather was a sober man though, and when it passed to him, he put it in a box, wrapped the whole thing up in muslin and put it in his attic. There it stayed, coming first to my mother, and then to me. I remember my mother showing it to me once, when I was little, but she immediately put it away again afterwards for safety. I'd forgotten all about it until last month, when I finally went through my grandfather's things. It's nice, but it holds little meaning for me. It deserves to be with someone who would treasure it again."

Miss Miller nodded. "I can understand that. What is the price of such a wonder?"

The man named a rather startling figure.

"That's a fair price for a functioning piece of its age," Zelma said.

"Excuse us one moment," Miss Miller said to the man, and pulled Zelma aside. "I can't comment on its actual age, but that fellow is definitely not being entirely honest with you. I strongly suggest demanding some tangible evidence of his story before paying that price."

"You're such a cynic, Mary."

"Not at all. I'm saying that based entirely on obvious evidence."

Why does Miss Miller disbelieve the man?

HINT

DISPOSITION

The Hero

I t had taken less than twenty-four hours for Clark Allison to go from just another blind hobo to being the toast of the city. He'd been the nearest person around when little Alice Wilkins had fallen into the boating lake at the bottom of the park. Despite having lost his eyesight twelve years before as a soldier, he'd leapt straight into the water without a second thought, found his way to her by her screams, and retained the presence of mind to bring her safely back to shore. The *Tribune* had run a tiny piece on the affair last night, and suddenly Allison was the man of the moment.

Reuben Marley, Josh's editor, was quick to set up an interview. "You're meeting him at the boating lake kiosk in half an hour," Marley declared.

Josh was quick to object, raising his bandaged right wrist.

Marley cut him off almost as soon as he opened his mouth. "I don't care about your sprain. Stop whining. If you still can't write, take Matthews with you. He can take your damned notes for you. Might as well have him get a photo or two as well, just in case, but tell him not to get his hopes up. We're running an image of the girl. Make yourself *useful*, man. I don't pay you to be decorative."

Sighing, Josh went to find his photographer. A hectic forty minutes later, he and Adam Matthews were outside the kiosk at the boating lake. The guy in the booth pointed them to a nearby

bench. On it sat a weather-beaten man
of broadly indeterminate age. His hair,
clothes and beard looked surprisingly
good, given his situation, but he
was wearing dark glasses and
carrying a white cane.

Josh went over
to him, Adam
following behind.
"Mr Allison?" he
said.

"Afternoon,
gentlemen," Allison
said. His voice
certainly sounded the
part, a mix of ground
glass and phlegmy
rattles. "You'll be
from the *Sentinel*,
I presume?"

"That's us. My name is
Josh Cole, and this is my photographer,
Adam Matthews."

"A pleasure." Allison stood, shook
hands with Adam, and nodded politely
to Josh in lieu of a handshake. "You find
me in unusual circumstances. I'm told I

look positively presentable today, thanks to your colleagues at the *Tribune*. I certainly haven't smelled this good in the best part of five years."

"What can you tell me about your life?" Josh asked.

Over the course of the next fifteen minutes, Allison outlined a poor boy's childhood, a stint in the army, the accident that had cost his sight, his discharge, and the depression that had led to first alcoholism and then destitution. He was perfectly frank about his flaws, and about how he'd expected to die when he hit the streets—hoped to, even. Adam scrawled notes quickly in a tangled hand that Josh despaired of ever deciphering, and Josh made the appropriate noises of interest and concern in the right places.

Then they moved on to the previous day's events. "I've been coming here since I cut the drink down," he told them. "I like to listen to the water lapping against the walls of the lake, and the noises of the birds. It's easy to imagine I'm looking at it. The people you hear are happy and relaxed, too. So much nicer than in the streets. I get by on the little bits and bobs they leave me. Yesterday, I was just sitting here when I heard the girl running, and then I heard the splash, and the screams. I didn't even think about it. I did what anyone would have done—I leapt in, swam over to her, and helped her to the side. Yeah, okay, I can't see anything, but it's not as if a boating lake is going to have crocodiles in it."

The rest of his story was familiar territory—grateful parents offering a night in a cheap hotel, a bystander who knew a reporter, and so on. "I'm hoping this might be a second chance for old Clark Allison," he said. "It was the drink that brought me down here. Without it, maybe I can find a way out of the gutter. Plenty of jobs a blind man can do, and you newspaper folk have been quite generous by a beggar's standards."

"It certainly makes for a heart-warming tale," Josh said to Adam as they made their way back out of the park. "He's no more blind than you are, but I don't think RM needs to know."

Why does Josh doubt Clark Allison's blindness?

HINT
ACTIONS

Under Attack

When Olivia Breeden entered the restaurant, she looked distinctly unhappy. Noticing Miss Miller at a window-side table, she waved off the waiter and made her way over.

"Thank you for meeting me at such short notice, Mary," she said, sitting down. "I hope you don't mind me imposing. I just can't make any sense of this, and Bonnie absolutely insists you're the person to talk to."

"Not at all," Miss Miller replied. "I'm always happy to do what I can." She poured herself some more tea while the waiter took Olivia's order for a coffee. Once the man had left, she smiled encouragingly. "Why don't you tell me the problem, my dear?"

"It's my husband. Philip is a wholesaler of vegetable and fruit, primarily. He and his partner Monroe employ ten men, four of whom are drivers, and their books are full. Business has been good for the last couple of years. People seem to be eating more fresh produce than they were five years ago. In fact, there is some nasty gossip . . . But I'm getting ahead of myself."

Miss Miller nodded encouragingly.

"Philip works until 6pm. He's very punctual about it. Two nights ago, he was leaving the yard when he was attacked. The fellow must have been hiding in the yard, because he came at Phil from behind, but luckily he'd heard a scuffle and was turning to look, and the first knife-thrust missed." She shuddered. "I can barely believe the words coming out of my mouth. The fellow tried to stab him in the back! Phil grabbed the man's arm, yelling, and they wrestled for a moment. Then he threw Phil to the ground, and ran off."

"My word," Miss Miller said.

"Well yes, quite," said Olivia. "The whole thing was a terrible shock to him. He remembers bits of it—the chap was a couple of inches taller, wearing a shirt and jacket like anyone else, and had dark hair—but mostly it was the knife that caught his attention, as I'm sure you can imagine. The police were prompt, but discouraging. I think they've decided it was just a random mugging."

"Did anyone else see anything?"

"Nothing useful, no. Monroe heard Phil shout, and saw the tail-end of the scuffle, but he never got a look at the man's face. All he could add was that the chap's tie was blue. A couple of the men were in the warehouse and heard the yell too, but by the time they got to the gate all they got to see were the fellow's heels. So between the four of them, the best we could do was that he was about six foot two, with dark hair. That was when the policeman's interest flickered and died."

"You mentioned gossip, Olivia."

"Oh, yes. It's been worrying me. Phil has heard people say that criminal gangs are trying to muscle in on the fruit and veg business, because it has been so profitable. It seems difficult to imagine that men with guns would want to bother taking over vegetable distribution, but I really don't know what to think."

"Fruit and veg could be a useful cover for distributing other things," Miss Miller said thoughtfully. "And could also dovetail quite nicely with smuggling. It's not impossible. Has anyone approached your husband about selling the business?"

"Not that I know of. He'd never sell it, though. His grandfather started the company, and his father brought in Monroe's uncle. Phil isn't going anywhere."

"Maybe that's the problem," Miss Miller said. "You should really get the police to have a nice long chat with your husband's partner about the attack."

Why does Miss Miller suspect Monroe's involvement?

HINT

LINES

A Politician's Tale

Handsome, charming, well-bred and ambitious, Alexander Hickman was a perfect political candidate, which was undoubtedly why he was a rising star of the local scene. He'd quickly been hailed as the new blood that was going to upset the established order, and his base of supporters was both wide and deep. Plenty of lesser figures had grand hopes for the places his coat-tails might sweep them to.

The main stumbling block in Hickman's road to power was the local incumbent, Emerson Woodey. Equally charming, well-bred and ambitious, but seventy rather than forty, what Woodey lacked in youthfulness, he made up for in connections. In public, he took pains to treat Hickman with pleasant, slightly patronizing bonhomie, like an uncle encouraging a gauche nephew. In private, it was said that he had a picture of Hickman placed against a wooden board so that he could throw knives at it.

When someone tried to assassinate Hickman in the opera house restrooms, the region's news went into a feeding frenzy. At the *Sentinel*, politics were Martin Houston's beat, but the story was big enough that the editor put Josh on it as well, to cover the criminal aspects.

That afternoon, Josh took his photographer, Adam, and met Hickman at the venue's bar. The man stood up as they approached.

"Mr. Cole, it's a pleasure to meet you. I'm a big fan of your work. I loved your takedown of Colin Andrews." He shook Josh's hand warmly. "And you must be Adam Matthews. You've got a great eye for composition, Mr. Matthews. The *Sentinel* is lucky to have you. Please, have a seat. I was just about to have them open me a bottle of wine." As Josh and Adam sat, Hickman waved over a waiter, and ordered a bottle of Château d'Yquem '69. "It's a little younger than I am, but not by much," he told them. "One of my best recent discoveries. I suppose you're keen to hear about that nasty business last night."

"Very much so," Josh said.

"Well, the facts are reasonably straightforward. I shan't embellish. It was during the Act Two break. I'd ordered some drinks, and then decided I ought to make use of the facilities while I had the chance. It was empty when I went in, which ought to have tipped me off that something was funny, but the implications missed me." The waiter arrived and presented a cork, which Hickman sniffed and nodded to. "I was just at the sink afterwards when, in the mirror, I saw a stall door open quietly behind me and, to my horror, a small gun-barrel protruded, aimed square at the middle of my back. It looked like the sort of thing you might find in the purse of an independently minded lady, if you know what I mean."

Josh nodded, and took a sip of his wine. It was excellent.

"Well, I'm not proud to say that I immediately threw myself to the floor. There was a quiet crack followed immediately by running footsteps and the door closing. I got back to my feet, and went to alert the management, but whoever the attacker was, he got away."

"You didn't see his face?"

"No. I caught a tiny glimpse of a pale moon-shape behind the gun, but the stall was only open a sliver. We asked around afterwards, but no one noticed anyone exiting the room. The police have been over everything of course, but they haven't found anything useful."

"Did you have any warnings beforehand that your life was in danger?"

Hickman nodded gravely. "There had been some threats. My campaign manager was worried, but I'm not. I love this country, and am not shy of risking my life to serve it. One of my staff came to me with a wild story about organized criminals liking the way that the system currently works and being averse to change, but I absolutely

refuse to believe that a man like Emerson Woodey would ever stoop to an accommodation with men like Benny Lucas. It's a truly ridiculous suggestion. I fired the man, of course."

"Of course," Josh agreed.

Hickman talked on for a while about his refusal to be cowed, his plans for bringing wealth and prosperity to the city, his lovely family, and so on. Occasionally, Josh managed to interject a question. After the wine was finished, Hickman showed them the restroom in question. Adam took photographs of the restroom doors, of the huge gilded mirror whose pristine cleanliness had saved the politician's life, of the stall barred off with police warning signs, and of Hickman looking bravely resolute. Finally, they escaped, leaving Hickman to talk to the *Chronicle*'s Verne Handley.

"He had a lucky escape," Adam said, as they got into a taxi.

"The whole story is utter nonsense," Josh said. "The question is, what is Marley going to do about it?"

Why does Josh doubt Hickman?

HINT

BULLET

Robbery at Bisbury's

The manager of Bisbury's Office Supplies was named Thomas Lane. A tall, thin man with a long jaw, he was pacing up and down his office, wringing his hands. Inspector Parnacki focused on the man's desk instead, which made for less strain on the eyes.

"You said that the robbery was well-timed," the inspector prompted.

Lane nodded. "Yes. The night before the last Friday in the month is when we have the most cash in the safe. There's money for both weekly wages and monthly salaries, as well as cash-only suppliers. On top of that, we've had a successful promotion on oak accoutrements this week, and there was a reasonable receipt from the floor. This is a total disaster."

He gestured at the safe, which hung open and empty. It was built high into the office wall, behind a framed, chest-high certificate of sales competency. A straight-backed office chair sat beneath it, a twin to the one that the inspector currently occupied in front of Lane's desk. Tall cabinets for filing stood along the opposite wall. Lane paused for a pregnant moment. "I was at home with my wife and children, incidentally."

"Do any members of staff know how to open the safe?"

Lane laughed bitterly. "Of course! All of them! Head office policy is that cash is not allowed to stay in the registers any longer than is necessary, to deter hold-ups. So everyone knows how to store money in there. The key is in my desk drawer. I lock it at night, but obviously that wasn't sufficient."

The drawer had been jimmied open easily, and now sat, splintered, on top of the desk. The key was still in the safe.

"If you had to guess whether one of them had robbed you—" Parnacki said.

"Reynolds," Lane said quickly. "He's just too cheerful and

good-looking to be working somewhere like this. He has to be up to something."

Parnacki nodded. "Is there somewhere I could talk to the staff?"

The manager sagged. "If you really want to. I'm not sure I advise it, though. One gets what one is allowed to pay for. Use this office. It's not as if it'll still be mine this evening anyway—I'll be sacked for this. I'll fetch them for you. One at a time, I assume?"

"Thank you. That's very kind."

Gene Reynolds was a tall, well-chiselled man with a ready smile and a somewhat theatrical air. If the robbery had dampened his spirits, he hid it well. "I left at 5.30 yesterday as usual," he said, "and went into the city. I met up with my lady friend, and then we saw a play, *The Wizard of Oz*. My Adele sure did love the cow, Imogene. Made her night. Afterwards, we retired for the evening, and that's all there is to say."

Henry Tyson was a brooding man of about Lane's height, with a widow's peak and a surprising beard that came to a sharp point several inches below his chin. It made him look as if he were about to whisk a dove out of a sleeve. "I was in my lodgings last night," he declared. "Eight of us have rooms at Mrs. Free's Boarding House. We are, all of us, working men. Unlike some, I do not despise our condition, but I look forward to the day when progress makes the brutality of menial work inefficient." He looked meaningfully at the inspector. "I was in the common room all evening, and my bedroom all night, as Mrs. Free's terrifyingly acute hearing will attest."

Finally, Marius Morse was a very small, punctilious man in his twenties with a handshake not unlike gripping a dead rat. "Last night was like every other," he said. "I live with my mother. My father died a decade ago, and his absence wears on her. I am at home every working night by six-twenty, and remain there until I have finished my breakfast—I leave at eight-fifteen in the morning, to be exact. I allow that I am sometimes out as late as ten-thirty on a Friday or Saturday night, but yesterday was neither."

After Morse had departed, Lane returned. "You've now met all my scintillating assistants. Genuine characters, each and every one, in the very worst sense of the word. I won't miss them one whit."

"Perhaps you could show one of them back in, Mr. Lane," said the inspector. "I just have a few more questions for him."

Who does Parnacki suspect, and why?

HINT

POSITION

Murder in the Alley

ntoinette Edwards was a pretty, vivacious seamstress who didn't come home one night. Her body was found the next morning in an alley behind a large department store in the centre of the city, a couple of blocks from a dance hall she typically frequented. Josh first heard of the murder from his police contact, Pete. The *Sentinel* was always interested in the murders of attractive girls. Any more information about the crime was still being kept under wraps, so Josh copied down the addresses of family and friends and went to look into the story's potential.

Antoinette still lived with her parents, so Josh's first port of call was the family home. A burly young man answered the door, and slammed it so hard when Josh identified himself that if he hadn't jerked his foot out of the way, he might have had a toe broken. Fortunately, there were several friends on his list that he could talk to.

Julian McMahan, a twenty-eight-year-old accountant, was Antoinette's intended. The two had been a couple for almost eighteen months, according to Pete's notes. Josh found him at the soap manufacturing company where he worked. He was a good-looking man of medium height and build, and his suit was of a reasonably high quality.

"We'd been stepping out for eighteen months or so," Julian said. "We were going to get engaged, get married, grow old together. I was out with her last night. I'm not much of a dancer myself, but it was Toni's passion, so I was happy to make the effort. I had an early start today, so I left her there with her friend Eva around ten-thirty. I've done it a dozen times. I never dreamed she'd wind up in a dumpster. It's beyond horrible. If I'd just stayed . . . I'll never forgive myself."

Sherman Emmett, a twenty-two-year-old butcher, had known Antoinette since the first year of school. "Toni was basically my sister," he told Josh. "She was a sweet, lovely woman with a ready smile for everyone. I still don't really believe that she's gone. I remember sneaking out of class with her one sunny afternoon, so that we could go down to the river to throw bread to the ducks. We were nine,

maybe? That's how I think of her, even now. A happy little scamp with a bag of sandwich crusts and the biggest grin in the world. She adored Julian, you know. Would have done anything for him. She was just waiting for him to pop the question. I was so happy for her—he's a good catch."

Eva Giles, 24, worked at the same textile shop as Antoinette. Josh couldn't gain admission to the site, but when her husband Grady came to pick her up from work, he got the chance to speak to the pair of them. There was a noticeable likeness between the two women, a doll-like loveliness that they'd both shared. "We just saw her last night," Eva said. "It's unreal. Poor Tee. She was completely lovely. Jules left a short time before her, but I didn't think anything of that. I think he had to be up early. It never occurred to me that she might come to harm."

"Antoinette was a darling," Grady added. "We'll all miss her like anything."

Back at his desk that evening, Josh was flicking through his notes, trying to find something for a story other than a typical hagiography. Then it hit him—he knew who the murderer was. His mouth spread into a grin, and he went to have an urgent chat with his editor.

Who does Josh suspect of the murder, and why?

HINT
DETAIL

The Root Cellar

Rachel Collier was clearly out of sorts. She was normally an excellent companion for an afternoon of birdwatching, but today she was barely communicating, missing the most obvious specimens, and not even really taking notes. Finally, after an hour or so, Miss Miller pulled her aside.

"My dear, whatever is wrong?"

"I'm sorry," Rachel said, sighing. "My thoughts are elsewhere, Mary. I was burgled last Tuesday."

"Oh, I am sorry. If you'll forgive me asking, how bad was it?"

"They cleared me out completely. Anything even slightly valuable and feasibly portable is gone. It's all insured, but you know how insurers are. Besides, most of it had personal significance."

"The police—" Miss Miller began.

Rachel shook her head. "No idea, no. The learned assessment of the sergeant they sent over to look around was

'Probably won't see none of that again, Missus.' Not exactly a great comfort."

"Oh, that's unhelpful of him. What a shame. Were you at home at the time?"

"We were out all day, actually. Got home late. The police were already there. Teresa, the maid, was down at the market. She got back and found the chaos, and went for help. Mr. Digweed, the handyman, was out in the shed servicing the boiler. He didn't hear a damned thing, not even the police turning up or us coming home."

"I suppose they broke a window to get in?"

"No. They came in through the root cellar. Well, I say 'they'. I assume it was they, given how much they carried off. Anyway, it seems as if they must have found the key."

Miss Miller frowned. "Found the key?"

"Yes. The gardener, Barry, lost his root cellar key the best part of six months ago. He came and told me the day it happened—he'd been out in the woods or some such, and noticed it missing when he got back. We cut him a new one, and didn't think much of it. But the thieves left the key in the cellar door, and both his and ours are accounted for. So it must be the lost one."

"That's a blow."

"Yes. Mark thinks the insurance will try to use it to weasel out of paying."

"I wonder why they left the key."

Rachel shrugged. "Didn't need it any more, and couldn't be bothered to close up behind them, I suppose. One last little slap, as if their contempt wasn't obvious enough." She fished around in her pocket, and pulled out a simple and perfectly regular-looking brushed iron key. "This is it. The police gave it back to me this morning. Said they were done with it, and I might as well have it, as if I wanted some sort of peculiar souvenir. Probably why I'm in such a state today."

"I totally understand, my dear," Miss Miller said. "I'm not in the least bit surprised you're not your normal self. I'm very sorry this has happened to you. Do you have any suspicions whether anyone of your acquaintance might be involved in this business?"

"You mean one of the staff? It did occur to me that the robbery was well-timed, but that hardly requires collusion. It would be easy enough to have a boy watching the place who could inform them when the time seemed opportune. I'm not entirely sure I could bear having to suspect one of our employees on top of everything else."

"The thing is," Miss Miller said. "I'm afraid that the evidence suggests you need to do exactly that."

Who does Miss Miller suspect, and why?

HINT

KEY

The Banana Trade

Carlos Reagan was a small-time smuggler who mainly peddled rum. He and his partner, Ivoire Marks, had remained at liberty primarily because nobody had been able to spare the time to gather evidence against them. Other issues were always more pressing—until Marks turned up dead near a dingy bar the pair frequented.

"Thank you for coming in, Mr. Reagan," Inspector Parnacki said. Carlos Reagan was a ferrety little man with a cheap suit and an indifferent haircut. Apart from the hard set to his eyes, he looked like a market trader.

"Yeah, well, I'm always real happy to help the law, officer."

"What was the nature of your relationship with Mr. Marks?"

"We was partners and friends. Known each other for seven years, been working together for five. He was a good man to have beside you in a brawl."

"Do you get in a lot of brawls?"

"Of course not," Reagan said. "It's just one of them figures of speech. We're strictly legitimate businessmen."

"And what business is that?"

"Importing bananas. The folks do love their bananas. Good news for us."

"Indeed. When was the last time you saw Mr. Marks?"

"We had a few drinks at the Olive Grove on Tuesday night."

"That was the night of the murder?"

"Yeah." He paused. "I saw it happen."

Parnacki leaned forward. "You did? Why didn't you report it yourself?"

Reagan sighed, looking shame-faced. "I just ran, officer. I figured he was coming after me too. I been laying low. Found your man's note this morning, when I went home for some stuff. That's when I decided that maybe the smart play was to come to see you."

"If you can help us find the killer, you'll have nothing to worry about."

"Here I am, ain't I?"

"So please, talk me through the events of Tuesday night."

"Well, like I said, we were at the Olive Grove on Sotton Street. We hung out there a lot. Ive and me, we were talking casually about our next shipment, uh, of bananas, and where we were going to offload them. Mainly, we were passing the time. We left about eleven, I suppose. I told Ive to wait out front for me a minute, because, well, I spotted someone I wanted to have a word with. A girl. Rebecca, her name is. So she and I, we go into the alley round the side of the bar, so as not to clog the pavement, like."

"Rebecca," Inspector Parnacki said. "Does she have a surname?"

"I dunno. I guess."

"She's not much of a friend, then. What business did you have with this girl?"

"I, uh, I just wanted to talk to her, you know?"

"No, I don't know."

Reagan slumped in his seat, and sighed heavily. "Look, I'm trying to be helpful here, officer. What's with the inquisition? Rebecca, she can be real friendly, if you get her in the right mood. I wanted to see if maybe I could find a way to help her be in the right mood. I wanted a bit of friendly company. That's all."

"Very well," Parnacki said, making a note. "Please continue."

"Okay. Good. Well, I was talking to Rebecca when I saw Minor coming up the street towards Ive."

"Minor?"

"Minor Cochran. He's a . . . well, he's someone we know a little. He's in imports as well."

"Ah yes," the inspector said. "We are familiar with Mr. Cochran."

"Right. So I didn't pay much attention. Like I said, we kinda know him. The next thing I know, there's a flash of steel, and Ive is falling flat on his face. Blood started pooling, way too quick to be something you could come back from. Meanwhile, Minor has turned around and is walking away from the bar again, casual as you like. So I hoofed it down the alley, and went to find a bottle of whiskey and a nice, anonymous hotel to sack out in."

"Can you think of any reason Mr. Cochran would have to kill Mr. Marks?"

Reagan shrugged. "Nothing personal I know of. I figure he wants to expand, get rid of the competition. That's why I been hiding out."

"The banana import competition?"

"That's right. It's a tough business."

"Apparently so," said Parnacki. "Carlos Reagan, I'm arresting you for the murder of Ivoire Marks."

Why does Inspector Parnacki suspect Reagan of being the murderer?

HINT

VISION

Death at Parrott's

Workplace deaths weren't particularly newsworthy, for the most part. Many professions were surprisingly dangerous, and no company was fond of having the papers run stories about their employees dying. It frequently made for legal complications, and the readers weren't all that interested anyway.

A stockman being hacked down with the company fire-axe was a totally different proposition. Josh was on his way to Parrott's Gifts and Delights almost as soon as Pete at the police station had hung up the phone.

When he arrived at Parrott's, Josh found the nearest worker, and called him over.

"Can I help you?" the guy asked.

"Joshua Cole, from the *Sentinel*. Could I have a moment of your time to talk about this morning's events?"

"You boys work fast. If I talk to you, I could get in trouble with the boss . . ."

Josh smiled, and handed over a wad of bills. "I can keep your name out of it."

" . . . but I'd be glad to help, Mr. Cole. The people need to know the truth, right?"

"Absolutely."

The guy, who was named Albin Gregory, gave Josh a thorough run-down of events. The dead man, a warehouse worker, was named Royce Murphy. He was well liked at Parrott's, and had been there for a decade or more. He'd been killed by a single blow to the chest from the company's own fire-axe. The murderer had also attacked another staff member, a junior salesman named Johnny Brendan, smashing him over the head before making his escape. When Brendan came round, he raised the alarm.

The attack had apparently happened while most of Parrott's workers were dealing with a delivery from Felder & Sons, a toy wholesale firm who'd been a long-time supplier of Parrott's. The delivery was brought round by an unfamiliar driver who'd said that the usual Felder & Sons driver, named Carter, was off sick. Gregory and his colleagues strongly suspected that there was a link. The manager of Parrott's, a younger man called Jason Samples, was not coping well. According to Gregory, he'd already been depressed thanks to a recent spate of thefts. He had left the office at midday, smelling strongly of whiskey, and had not returned.

Josh digested Gregory's information for a bit, and gave him a bit more cash to keep him around for a few minutes longer. "You said the murderer used the company fire-axe? Is it somewhere obvious, then?"

Gregory nodded. "Sure. It's kept on a stand just inside the warehouse's side door. We all use it for stuff all the time. It's real obvious." He paused. "Never imagined it'd get used on a guy, though."

"What did you think of this new Felder's driver?"

"I didn't get to meet him. I was in the warehouse with Winston, breaking down old crates to make some space. He was chopping, and I was stacking. We finished up in time to go help move the last of the delivery, but Felder's were already gone. While Winston was putting the axe back, Taylor told me about the new guy. Said he seemed like a decent enough sort, and that he sounded like he was from further north. Dale, I think Taylor said his name was. Taylor's a shrewd guy, most of the time. But it wouldn't be difficult to hide among the Felder stock and slip out while we were all busy with boxes. It's not as if we take delivery of more than a quarter of the stuff. They were gone by eleven."

"And Johnny, the guy who found the victim. How's he?"

"They took him to St. Anne's, just in case, but he seemed to be okay. Just a bit groggy."

Josh nodded. "Then I better get over there. Thanks for your time, Albin. You've been a great help."

Finding Johnny Brendan at St. Anne's was no great problem. Josh was well-known in the hospital, and kept everyone friendly with regular fruit baskets for the nurses in the trauma and recovery wards. He was pointed to a room with a policeman outside. A flash of his badge and the price of an evening out proved more than enough to get him through the door.

At first glance, Brendan looked perfectly fine. He had a bandage on his head, but his eyes were lively, and his skin tone nice and healthy.

"You must be the hero who risked his life this morning," Josh said as he closed the door.

"I guess I must," Brendan said, with a smile. "You with the papers?"

"That I am," Josh said, showing his card. "Joshua Cole, with the *Sentinel*. Can you tell me what happened this morning?"

"It was crazy. I saw Felder's arriving at ten forty-five, so I went down to check their manifest. I had to check old stock first, so I went into the warehouse and turned a quiet corner, and there was Murphy, lying on the floor. He had an axe buried in his chest, and was making horrible noises. I've never heard anything like it." He shuddered. "I froze for an instant. There was a noise behind me, and a burst of blinding pain. I remember sinking to the ground, and seeing a short, burly man with tousled hair.

I didn't see his face. Everything went dark. What felt like a moment later, I staggered to my feet, and started yelling for help. Turned out that was ten past eleven. Then everything was a blur of police and ambulances. I told the cops what had happened, and then I was brought here. Luckily, the doctors think I escaped any real injury."

Josh flattered Brendan some more, and left to put an urgent call to Pete. "I can tell you the identity of the Parrott's murder," he said. "Trade you for a spot at the arrest?"

Who does Josh suspect and why?

HINT

DELIVERY

The Missing Specimen

Matthew Arrowood held doctorates in both chemistry and biology. A former professor of Miss Miller's, he'd long since given up teaching. He remained an active amateur scientist, and from time to time, helped her out with the analysis of puzzling substances or remains. He was by nature a calm and studious man, so she was rather surprised, one Tuesday morning, to find him in his garden in a state of some upset.

He smiled at her absent-mindedly when he saw her approaching. "Hello, Mary. You'll have to forgive me if I seem a little out of sorts today."

"Is everything alright?" she asked.

"I seem to have mislaid a rather important body."

"I beg your pardon?"

He sighed. "A passenger pigeon, to be precise. Well preserved by a competent taxidermist, no more than fifteen years ago."

"I haven't seen a flock of passenger pigeons in more than twenty years," Miss Miller said. "That's quite a prize."

Matthew nodded. "It is indeed. I purchased this one at a
blind auction of ornithological specimens last week—for quite
a considerable sum, too—and took delivery yesterday. She was
there last night, before I turned in at ten. A few minutes ago, I
discovered her missing. I was just glancing around the garden, to
make sure that she hadn't been dumped out here as a prank."

"I doubt anyone would break into your house in the dead of
night just to leave their prize in the garden."

"Well, no, and indeed they did not. It was a very feeble hope. I
suppose I should contact the police."

"Is there anything else missing?"

"Not that I can see, no."

Miss Miller nodded. "Who knew that the pigeon was in your
keeping?"

He paused, thoughtfully. "The auction house. But I don't see
an auctioneer's lad stealing a bird when there are more easily sold
treasures available even in my home."

"I see what you mean," she said. "But maybe I should drop by
Ailey's anyway, and see if I can find your delivery lad for a word
or two. If nothing else, he might give us something to go on."

"That's very kind of you, my dear girl. Thank you."

"A pleasure. In the mean time, you should go ahead and inform
the police of the theft."

"I shall. Thanks again."

An hour later, Miss Miller was sitting in the office of Bertram
Ailey, proprietor of Ailey's Auctions. He was in his fifties, with an

unruly thatch of salt and pepper hair and a deeply seamed face.

"Thank you for agreeing to see me, Mr. Ailey," she said.

"How may I be of assistance?"

"You sent a purchase to Dr. Arrowood yesterday. Do you happen to know who made the delivery?"

"Oh, yes, from the bird auction. I don't know who took it down off-hand, no. I'll look it up for you." He paused, and looked concerned. "Was there a problem? Were the goods damaged?"

Miss Miller smiled. "Oh, no, it's nothing to worry about. I was coming past, so Dr. Arrowood asked me to follow up on something the fellow told him. Not a business matter."

Ailey gave her an uncertain glance. "I see. Well, that was . . ." He riffled through a ledger. "It was one of Ronnie's drops yesterday. Ronnie Griffith. It's lunchtime, so he should be in the yard somewhere. He's the fair-haired one."

"Thank you very much," Miss Miller said. "You've been very helpful."

There were several young men out in the yard, talking together. One of them did indeed have fair hair. Miss Miller called him over.

"Mr. Griffith, my name is Miss Miller. Do you mind if I ask you a couple of questions about a delivery?"

Griffith peered at her suspiciously. "I suppose."

"You made a delivery to Dr. Arrowood yesterday, I believe."

"Yes. So what?"

Miss Miller forced herself to smile pleasantly. "Was there anything strange about the delivery?"

"No. I took a package to an old man, who signed for it. That's all."

"So you didn't notice anything odd?"

Griffith glowered at her. "I don't like your tone." He turned back towards the group he'd just left. "Mel! What was I doing last night?"

One of the young men turned, grinning broadly. "Failing to drink me under the table. You got so drunk I had to pour you back up the stairs of your rooms, and your landlady gave me a right telling-off."

One of the others laughed. "Yeah, you were drinking like a sailor, Ronnie boy."

"See?" Griffith demanded. "I was dead drunk, and I'm paying for it today, and that's my business. Whatever you're worried about, I didn't do it."

"I'm sorry to have wasted your time," Miss Miller said.

A few minutes later, she found a public telephone, and called Matthew. "Have the police arrived yet? Well, when they do, tell them to focus on the auction house."

Why does Miss Miller think the auctioneers are involved?

HINT

OPPORTUNITY

The Printer's Wife

Pearline Dailey was found dead one cold Friday evening in a small residential street near her home. The murder weapon, a hunting knife, was wiped clean and left next to the body. There was no purse on the body, so initially a random mugging was suspected, but it turned out that she'd just left it at home when she went out. Interest then moved to her estranged husband, Lambert Dailey. On Saturday lunchtime, Inspector Parnacki decided to call on the man.

Lambert Dailey lived in a pleasant district about half a mile from his wife's apartment. His house was a fairly new-looking two up, two down with a modest but tidy front garden. The night's frost still lingered on the grass. The inspector went up to the front door, which was painted green, and knocked on the door. There were some thumps and clangs from deep in the house, and after a minute or so, a somewhat dishevelled man in his late thirties opened the door.

"Mr. Dailey?" asked the inspector.

The man nodded pleasantly. "Yes."

"My name is Inspector Parnacki. I wonder if I might ask you a few questions?"

"Of course. Poor Pearl." His face crumpled for a moment. "Please, come in, get out of the cold." Dailey showed the inspector through to the delightfully warm lounge. "Now, how may I be of assistance?"

"I understand you and your wife had some difficulties in your relationship," Parnacki said.

"You could say that." Dailey sighed. "Pearl was a splendid woman in many ways, but over the last few years, she and I had simply grown apart. We found it difficult to tolerate each other's little foibles calmly. It became obvious that remaining in close proximity was emotionally damaging to us both, so I rented her an apartment where she could have her own space. At first, we made an effort to at least go out to meals together regularly, but even that had fallen by the wayside somewhat. My work is quite demanding, and it makes schedules difficult."

"What is it you do, Mr. Dailey?"

"I'm a printer. The nature of the business is that sometimes you spend a week sitting on your hands and fretting, while other times you're working to midnight for thirty days in a row. This week, I've been at a trade fair a couple of hundred miles away. If my secretary hadn't known my hotel and room number, I'd still be there, but as soon as I heard about Pearl I made my apologies and left. In fact, I only got back about five minutes before your arrival. I was down in the basement turning the gas back on when you rang."

"A trade fair?"

"Yes, the book fair, in Barton. I do quite a lot of work with publishers, so I make a point of going to all the fairs, making sure they know me and remember my name. It's very important to make friendly contacts. That's one of the things Pearl never really understood."

"So I dare say you had several meetings yesterday?"

Dailey nodded. "Of course. Yesterday afternoon, I was with Taylor Free and Martin Houston, who run a company out the other side of Barton. We discussed calendars for a while, and then I took them out for drinks. I'm afraid we got rather tipsy, but it was a merry time."

"I see. Can you think of anyone who might have wanted to harm your wife?"

"I've been asking myself the same question. There was a man . . . A former worker of mine, name of Hayden Killian. He was, well, odd. Unsociable. Weird. He met Pearline at a couple of office events, and was obviously very taken with her. I let him go early last year, because he made the other staff nervous. He seemed to take it well enough, but who knows?"

The inspector jotted some notes in his pad. "I'm afraid I'm going to have to ask you to come down to the station for further questioning, Mr Dailey."

Why does Inspector Parnacki suspect Lambert Dailey?

HINT

DURATIONS

Death on the Steps

J osh Cole was in the courthouse to cover a high-profile assault case when a growing hubbub disrupted proceedings. Word quickly spread that someone had been shot just outside the building. Assault forgotten, Josh snatched up his pad and ran to investigate.

It didn't take long to find out what had happened. Clinton Tarwater, a prominent defence attorney, had been giving a statement on the courthouse steps regarding the "not guilty" verdict that his client, one Art Macinello, had just secured. Josh had been aware of the case, which wasn't very interesting. Macinello was one of Benny Lucas's boys, and obviously guilty, but he was equally obviously going to get off. The evidence was thin, and the guy Macinello had killed was another mobster, so no one really cared.

Except, of course, that now Tarwater was lying dead on the steps.

A number of people were milling around silently, so Josh took the opportunity to start finding out who they were.

Kate Sneed was an attractive woman in sharp clothing who looked significantly more distressed than most of the others there. "Yes, I knew Clint," she said unhappily. "We were . . . close, a couple of years ago. I haven't seen much of him since then. I was coming to the court for a different case, but when I saw him out here, I decided to wait and say hi after he'd said his piece.

Then he just jerked, and collapsed, and blood . . ." She fell silent, face twisting. "He didn't deserve this. He was a fun guy."

A tall, expensively dressed man hovering near the body turned out to be Karl Massey, a junior colleague of Clint's. "Mr. Tarwater was giving a short, prepared statement on the clear and proven innocence of Mr. Macinello when an unidentified assailant shot him in the chest, killing him instantly. That is all that I am able to share with you at this time. I speak for everyone at Proctor, Tarwater and Atkinson in condemning this senseless murder, and in offering our most sincere condolences to Mr. Tarwater's family."

Max Stanton was standing nearby, and described himself as a former client of Tarwater's. "I'm afraid I didn't see anything interesting, Mr. Cole. I meant to be here for the speech, but I was running late. As I got here, most of the people had already run away, and everyone remaining seemed in shock. It was clear enough what had happened, though. It's a real shame. Clint was an okay guy, you know? He did his best for me, and was always patient with my problems and complications. He could be a real terror on the courtroom floor, but he rarely got angry outside it. In fact, he was quite the charmer when he wanted to be. He's going to leave a big, Clint-shaped hole in the legal scene, that's for sure. It's a shame that loud truck was going past when he was shot—the killer must have got clean away when the group panicked."

"Tarwater was a mob shill, and his hands were drenched in blood." Mack Scott, the prosecuting attorney in the Macinello

case, was clearly still bitter. "I heard the fuss, and came out. I can't say I'm surprised. He died like he lived—a mobster in all but name. I don't condone murder of course, but if it had to happen to someone then there are worse targets that it could have been. I hope that his colleagues will take a lesson from his ridiculous death and think long and hard about the types of clients that they are prepared to take on."

Josh had only managed to get the name of one more guy—Ike Underwood—before the police finally locked the scene down and, having identified all the witnesses for further statements, dispersed the group remaining near the body. Josh didn't mind. He went back into the courthouse, found a public telephone, and called the station.

"Pete? It's Josh. Clinton Tarwater, the lawyer. You know him? Yeah, him. He's just been murdered, and I'm 99 percent sure I can tell you who did it."

Who does Josh suspect, and why?

HINT

POSITIONING

The Peacock Room

Miss Miller had been introduced to Therese Freshour at parties from time to time, and had found her pleasant, but she would hardly have called her a friend. So she was a little surprised to receive a visit from Therese one afternoon. She welcomed her into the drawing room, shooed Aubrey out from underfoot, and ordered refreshments for the pair of them. They exchanged pleasantries until the tea and biscuits arrived, discussing the similarities and

differences between birdwatching and gardening.

Once they were alone, Miss Miller looked at her visitor. "So, my dear. To what do I owe the unexpected pleasure?"

Therese looked slightly uncomfortable. "May I be frank with you, Mary?"

"Always."

"You have a certain reputation, you know."

Miss Miller arched an eyebrow. "Oh?"

"If one talks to people about irksome issues, your name comes up time and again as something of a panacea. The Boyers, with their icon. Mrs. Keeler. The Mattingley affair. It is said that you have the eyes of a hawk, and a mind like a steel trap."

"People are far too kind."

Therese didn't seem convinced. "Perhaps." She looked at her fingernails, and rubbed her thumb back and forth over them.

"But you have an irksome issue of your own, and you wonder if perhaps I can be of assistance."

"Yes."

"My dear, I'd be delighted to try," Miss Miller smiled. "I'm genuinely flattered. If I can shed any light, I'll be happy to do so."

"Thank you." Therese looked greatly relieved.

"Why don't you tell me about it? I'll wade in as questions occur to me."

"It was Wednesday. I'd been fussing over my dahlias for most of the afternoon. The rain finally drove me inside at about five. I read a magazine for a little while, hoping it would abate, but the dratted stuff didn't stop until gone eight. So after a while,

I gave up, and joined Hobart in a cocktail before dinner. He wasn't finding the newspapers any more diverting than I was my magazine."

Miss Miller nodded encouragingly.

"We ate at seven-thirty, and after dinner I settled down to read for an hour. Hobart toddled off to do some paperwork. His nephew Elijah, my sister-in-law's son, is staying with us for a few months. Jasmine wanted to get him away from a veritable coven of bad influences for a while. He's something of a law unto himself, though. He got back around half-past eight, declined any dinner, and took a large scotch to keep him company while he played patience on the dining room table. I decided to do a little work on a quilt I'm decorating. It's a heavy beast, so I called the maid, Zena, away from her cleaning to assist. Then, at half-past nine, the butler, Gregory, appeared and regretfully told me that there had been a break-in."

"Oh?"

"Yes. They smashed a skylight in the Peacock Room, up on the third floor. It's where we keep our oriental collection. Hobart and I dashed up there. The carpet was soaked through, and little fragments of glass had gone everywhere. They hadn't damaged any of the display cases, though. I assume they tied a rope to one of the stanchions on the roof to get down and back up. They took a number of pieces from in there, but the most important was a T'ang dynasty porcelain figurine. It was a gift from my uncle, and it's quite irreplaceable."

"I see. Do you have any idea when the break-in occurred?"

"Well, we can narrow it down to between about eight-fifty and nine-thirty. Zena dusts on the third floor after dinner, and everything was fine when she went through, which was about ten to nine. Gregory noticed some cold air when he left the kitchens just before half-past nine, and went hunting an errant open window. So it's somewhere between then. Zena was with me. Gregory was with Maxine and Mrs. Edwards in the kitchen. Elijah was playing cards, and Hobart was working. It seems impossible none of us noticed a window that size being broken, but there it is. The police seem quite baffled, and Lord knows I certainly am. Is there anything we're missing?"

"Actually, yes," Miss Miller said. "I've got a fairly firm idea of your culprit."

Who does Miss Miller suspect, and why?

HINT
PRESENCE

Blackwell's Boiler Company

A perfectly respectable manufacturer of boilers, Joseph Keith seemed an unlikely murder victim. However, he was found dead at midday in a small park a half-mile or so from his place of work with a knife sticking out of his side. A small, type-written note in his pocket listed that location, and a time of 11.30. Inspector Parnacki was unable to find any other obvious evidence on the body, so he packed his pipe and strolled over to the office address listed on the dead man's business card.

The office in question was surprisingly small, a set of rooms on the second floor of a building divided into small businesses. A sign on the door proudly declared it to be Blackwell's Boiler Company, so he went in.

A pleasant-looking young woman at a reception desk glanced at a clock, which showed the time as being quarter to one, and smiled up at him. "Mr. Calderon?"

"Inspector Parnacki," he replied. "I'm afraid I'm here about the murder of Mr. Joseph Keith earlier today."

All the blood drained from the woman's face, and she wailed something unintelligible. A moment later, a door opened, and a man in his forties appeared. The inspector explained his presence, and the man—Zachary Harris, Keith's business partner—ushered him into his office.

"I was afraid something like this might happen," Harris said, once he was over his initial shock. "Joe had arranged a major lunch meeting here today with a couple of property developers. Their names are Calderon and Justus. They appeared out of nowhere a couple of months ago, throwing money around and buying up chunks of the city. They've been here before, and I really didn't like them. They felt wrong. But they *really* want to buy our warehouse—they're offering three times the market value, and a new location to move to. The new place is inconvenient, but it's a lot of money. I didn't want to know, but Joe insisted we hear them out, test the waters, maybe see if they'd go higher. He went out to a meeting this morning, but he wouldn't tell me anything about it. Milicent might

know. She keeps both our appointment books. She's extremely efficient. Joe should have been back an hour ago. The lunch meeting is due to start in about five minutes, and I was getting nervous. Calderon and Justus really aren't men you stand up. In fact, I'd already told Millie that if Joe didn't appear and the guys arrived, she was to pretend I was out. Now he's dead. Why would they kill him? He was happy to sell. It's insane."

The inspector thanked Harris, and went to talk to the secretary, Millicent Lewelling. "I'm sorry about earlier," she told him. "It was such a horrible shock. Mr. Keith was a nice guy. I'm afraid I don't have any idea where he got to this morning, no. I didn't have anything in the book for him until this big lunch meeting at one. I wasn't actually here earlier, though. I was out arranging for the lunch spread—fancy sandwiches, a range of drinks, cakes, a couple of floral displays for the meeting room table, the full deal." She gestured to a stack of assorted boxes by her desk. "Mr. Keith really wanted to make a good impression on these guys. So I've been running around. When I got back, about an hour ago, I noticed that Mr. Keith had slipped out. I thought maybe he'd thought of some last finishing touch that he hadn't considered last night."

The door to the office opened, and a pair of tall, muscular men in expensive suits entered the office. They saw Inspector Parnacki standing there by the reception desk, and froze.

He nodded at them. "Messrs Calderon and Justus? Inspector Parnacki. May I have a word?" They reluctantly let him usher them into the meeting room and sat opposite him across the empty table. "I'm afraid Mr. Joseph Keith was killed this morning," he told them.

The two men exchanged shocked glances. Emotions flickered quickly over their faces—surprise, calculation, suspicion, fear—before their impassive masks slid back into place. The slightly smaller one nodded to his companion, and they both stood up again. "Mr. Justus and myself have been in well-documented meetings all day, Inspector," said the slightly taller of the two. "Good afternoon."

With that, they left the meeting room, and moments later, the office door slammed behind them.

Inspector Parnacki let them leave without protest. The killer's identity was perfectly obvious.

Who does Inspector Parnacki suspect and why?

HINT
AWARENESS

Joiner's Hill

As one of the steeper roads in the city, Joiner's Hill was no stranger to accidents. That morning's crash was spectacular by anyone's standards, however. A cart full of metalwork had come unhitched near the top of the hill, and then careened down it, over the main road, and straight into the side of a flour mill. Both the men on the cart had been flung clear of the wreckage, but while one had escaped with a broken leg, the other had died, impaled on a sharp spike of ornamental

metalwork. Josh Cole was on his way over there within forty seconds of the tip coming in, Adam Matthews and his camera in tow.

By the time Josh made it to the foot of Joiner's Hill, the traffic in the area had ground to a complete stop. The drivers were gone, but the wreckage was still there, apparently untouched. The police officers guarding the site knew Josh by sight, and let Adam through to photograph the metal-studded wall, the splintered cart, and the bloody cab. On the far side of the wreckage, a shaft of metal lay on a patch of blood-soaked pavement. While Adam took pictures, Josh confirmed with the officers in charge of the scene that it had been the metalwork that had killed the unlucky delivery man.

The next port of call was the Foundry, the place that the men had come from. It wasn't far, so Josh set off up Joiner's Hill, with Adam in tow. When they arrived, they discovered that the police had already notified the firm about the accident. A grim-faced worker took Josh and Adam to talk to the company manager, Addison Perry.

"This is a horrendous shock to all of us," Perry told them. "The men, Troy Morrison and Emerson Manning, have both been with the Foundry for years. We're like a family here, truly. Troy's death is a terrible, terrible loss. I can only imagine what his wife, Vena, is going through. This is the first fatal accident that the Foundry has had in more than thirty years, which is a significant feat for a company that deals in industrial and decorative metalwork. But we hold ourselves to the highest possible standards of both safety and production, which is why jobs here are so sought after."

"Quite," Josh said. "Have you had many cart accidents?"

"Never! We make our own fittings, of course, so we keep all our carts in top condition. I can't imagine how it came loose. Truly, it is a dark day. Troy and Emerson set off for Banks the Jewellers at around ten. Everything seemed perfectly normal. They're great friends, and were joking away merrily as they loaded the cart. Emerson's the driver, and a steadier pair of hands I've never known. We're extremely fortunate that he escaped serious injury. I want him to take all the time he needs to get well, though. There's no question of docking his pay or anything. We're supporting him to the very hilt."

Despite his best efforts, Josh couldn't persuade Perry to give him either Morrison or Manning's home addresses. After a while, he gave up, and decided to attempt to get them from Pete instead. Back at the office, he was in the process of dialling the station when a realization hit him. "Hey, Pete, it's me. The Joiner's Hill crash earlier was no accident. It was murder, and I can prove it."

Why does Josh think the crash was a murder?

HINTS
WRECK

Murder in Winter

February was, by and large, a rather quiet time for the homicide department. Murder rates usually spiked during the summer, and slowly declined through the winter, only rallying when spring came around. So when Madge Garland was found strangled in her own home, everyone leapt into action. By the time Inspector Parnacki was called in, a wide range of experts and other officers had arrived at the scene, and in some cases had already left again.

Officer Alonzo Pruitt was the first to arrive. "It took me about half an hour to get here. The snow had finally stopped, but the streets were still pretty chaotic. I needed a few minutes to actually find the path up to the house, too. The snow had blanketed everything. The husband reported the murder. He appeared to be in shock, and described finding his wife in the lounge, already dead. The back door was open. Several items of jewelry were missing, along with her purse. There weren't any footprints or other marks of disturbance in the snow around the house, which suggests that the murder occurred before the snow finished. That was around 5pm, I believe."

Pierre Steele was a forensic technician with the department. He'd performed an examination in situ before the coroner gave permission for the body to go to the morgue. "Victim was in her forties. Primary cause of death was strangulation," he said. "There were some other wounds that would suggest a short fight. The size of the bruises would fit with a male attacker. It's difficult to estimate the time of death, because the house is very cold. If the killer had closed the back door, I'd say some time in the morning—but, obviously, he didn't. We may be able to get a better idea later."

The victim's husband, Raleigh Garland, was in the kitchen of the house. He sat there numbly, wrapped in a large coat and clutching a mug of coffee, while people bustled around him. The inspector went to join him.

"My name is Inspector Parnacki. You must be Mr. Garland?"

"I've heard of you," Garland said. "You were in the paper. Are you really called Paddington?

"It's a nickname. May I ask you some questions?"

"Sure."

"Could you talk me through the events of this evening?"

"Okay. I work at Shuler Brothers, a financial institution in the city. It had been snowing, and the traffic was horrible by the time I escaped the group meeting, so it took me for ever to get home. It was half past six by the time I arrived. The place was dark, which seemed odd. I thought maybe Madge was napping. When I opened the door, I realized it was really cold inside. That's when I knew something was wrong. Madge is very particular. I called out, but there wasn't any answer. Then I found her lying on the floor of the lounge. I tried to wake her up, but she wouldn't wake up. She was so cold. She hates being cold. I could see she wasn't breathing. So I called for help. And then your man arrived, and then more people, and still more, and they took Madge away, and now you're here. That's it."

"Thank you, Mr. Garland. That's all for the moment."

He went in the hallway, and called Officer Pruitt over. "We need to get Mr. Garland down to the station," he said. "Come with me."

Why does Inspector Parnacki suspect Mr. Garland?

HINT

WEATHER

The Last Performance

Aloysius Gentry was always in the news. The flamboyant actor thrived on controversy, and made it a point to be seen with mysterious, beautiful women, high-profile politicians, and even known mobsters. If he wasn't sparking gossip with someone intriguing, he was being outspoken on controversial issues, or, if all else failed, slapping photographers. His biggest splash was his last, however—shot dead on stage, in the middle of a sell-out performance.

Philip Carter from the *Sentinel* had been to a prior staging of the show. He wasn't happy that the editor, Reuben Marley, had given the story to Josh Cole, but he grudgingly agreed to talk Josh through the fatal moment in the play. "There's a face-off between Dallas—that's Aloysius's character—and Israel, played by Coy Luskan. They're arguing over Alice, played by Idella Johnson. Israel pulls a gun on Dallas. The lights cut. There's a bang, and Alice screams, and when the lights come back on, Dallas is lying there dead, in a pool of blood that Aloysius tips from a bag when he lies down. It's the pivotal moment of the play. I hear that last night, no one realized Aloysius was actually dead until the scene change a couple of minutes later, when he didn't get up. He'd have loved that."

Pete at the station was able to confirm the manner of death. "He was definitely shot with a bullet. Sometimes a blank goes wrong, and that can be fatal, but this was a slug. A live round."

At the scene of the crime, Josh was met by the play's director, Arnolph Barker. "This was a tragic accident, Mr. Cole," Barker said. "Absolutely tragic. I don't want you distressing my cast any further."

"I understand completely," Josh said. "I'd never dream of intruding, or speaking to your people without your permission.

Of course, I can't get a clear picture of events without talking to them myself. For now—from the very sketchy information I've got so far—I'm thinking it looks a lot like murder. 'No Safety on the Stage of Death' has a nice ring to it."

Barker went pale. "You *wouldn't*."

"I'd much rather not," Josh smiled.

"Speak to them then, damn you. There's nothing to hide. I trust you'll clearly see that this was an accident. But if you throw my cast off their game, the *Sentinel* will never get access to my cast or shows again."

"I'll bear that in mind," Josh said. "Thanks for your time."

Coy Luskan, the villain of the piece, was more than happy to talk to Josh. "Poor Al was shot from the audience," he said. "I'm sure of it. It wouldn't be difficult to get the timing right to match with my shooting the prop gun. A few visits to the play, and he'd have it down pat. The music stops, there's a beat, and then bang! It's like clockwork. I thought the shot I fired sounded wrong. It can only be because there was a second shot!" His handwringing went on for several more minutes, but Josh didn't bother noting that down.

Idella Johnson was somewhat more restrained. "I know Coy claims there was another shot, but I definitely didn't hear one. I was off to the side, remember. Coy killed Aloysius all right. I just can't think *why*. Aloysius rubbed a lot of guys the wrong way—gals, too, although I'd never hurt a fly—but not Coy. They were genuinely good friends."

Henry Nichols was the prop handler. "Whoever shot Mr.

Gentry, it wasn't with the prop revolver. Mr. Luskan and I watched Mr. Grey, the prop manager, get it out of the locker, and I passed it to Mr. Luskan. Then he went on set. There's no way he'd have had time to chamber a real round in the dark and then shoot Mr. Gentry. There are no live rounds in the gun locker, just blanks, and if you look at our blanks, the difference is really obvious. On top of that, the cabinet is really secure." He gestured to a very sturdy metal cabinet against a wall. "Mr. Grey wears the only key around his neck, and you'd have to bend the doors to break into it. So it's impossible it was the prop gun, and that means it wasn't Mr. Luskan. His costume would have showed a second gun really clearly. Mr. Grey will tell you the same when he comes in."

"It's OK," Josh said. "I've already got a good idea of what happened."

Who does Josh suspect of killing Aloysius Gentry, and why?

HINT

ELIMINATION

The Widow

Polly Tuck, a young widow who lived in one of the poorer parts of town, was found dead following a loud argument in her home one evening. Examination of the home showed no signs of forced entry, and there didn't appear to be any theft. She died as a result of head trauma, but she had a number of other bruises and lacerations of varying ages and states of healing. Her former husband, Bill Tuck, had been a construction worker. His death had been the result of a fall while working, and had happened some two and a half years earlier. The couple had not had any children, and after his death, Polly had taken work as a waitress. Relatives characterized her as quiet but optimistic.

Initial interest focused on Polly's boyfriend, Sherman Clark, a former colleague of her dead husband. A burly man of thirty, he turned up to his interview with Inspector Parnacki quite drunk, with several days of stubble showing.

"Yeah, I had a few drinks," he said. "So what? It's not a crime. Polly was a good girl, most of the time. She knew what I liked, and made sure I got it. Never any lip from her. That's a rare quality in a girl. After Bill died, I made sure she was doing OK. Helped her get through it. We got close through that. I wouldn't never harm a hair on her pretty head. What? Bruises? She was clumsy, officer. That's all. Forever tripping up or banging herself on something. I'd tell her to be careful all the time, but somehow it never quite took. You know how it is. Tuesday night, I was down at the Parrot on Frith Street. Went there after work with some of the boys, to work off some steam. We stayed until they kicked us out at eleven."

Despite Clark's protestations, there was a witness to the attack. Alvin Mason, a thirty-eight-year-old store clerk, lived next door.

"I saw that big monster club her down. It was about eight on Tuesday night. I heard shouting start up from Polly's house again. That wasn't uncommon, but it sounded different this time. I worried about her, Inspector. She was a sweet, kind young woman, and she shouldn't have been involved with a man like that. She deserved better than another two-fisted drunk. I did my best to take care of her after her husband passed away, but she fell back into the same familiar old patterns. So, like I said, on Tuesday, it sounded worse than usual. I thought about calling for help. I wish to God I had. But I didn't. I bundled up warm, and went round to her house. The sitting room curtains were ajar, so I went up to the window, wiped off the condensation, and looked in. Clark was holding her by the throat, fist raised. Then he punched her out of his grip, and her head smacked into the fireplace. I gasped, and he turned, so I ran. I'm so ashamed. I ran and hid. I heard her door slam, and then a few minutes later, I went to check on her. She was already dead."

Faye Gibbs, an older woman, lived on the other side of Polly's house. "I heard them shouting over there, yes. I often does. It's sad, a pretty thing like that trapped with that kind of man. Just like her husband before him. Some people don't get to escape, I suppose. Anyway, it stopped, and I didn't think nothing more of it, not until your man was knocking on my door. Mostly we keep to ourselves, round here."

Reading his notes again, Inspector Parnacki sighed. It was a cruel waste, but at least the identity of the murderer was clear.

Who does Inspector Parnacki suspect and why?

HINT
WINTER

The Audacious Burglar

Nella Green turned, her heel crunching on the white gravel drive, and gestured at an empty bay window. A piece of tarpaulin had been fastened on the inside to stop the elements. "That's where he came in," she said. She sighed, and perched herself on the lip of her latest acquisition, a large electric fountain which flung curtains of water up towards a central display of naiads.

"Obviously nobody heard the window break," Miss Miller said, eyeing the window frame. Plenty of space to squeeze through there.

"We were all at dinner. The dining room is on the other side of the house, and Aldred and I had the Holberts over, and both of the maids were in attendance. I wouldn't expect Cook to hear anything from the kitchen even if the house were quiet. We might still have heard the glass break, but we'd lost power earlier, and all the gas lights were going. One forgets quite what a hiss they make. So we were talking away a bit more loudly than usual. It was all jolly festive, until we found the damage."

Miss Miller nodded. "Did he get a lot?"

"My bag, Emeline Holbert's bag, Aldred's medals, the wallet from Ewell Holbert's coat, a rather nice old carriage clock, and a small golden swan I received as a wedding present from Aldred's mother. It's immensely embarrassing, of course." Nella sighed.

"You said that the gardener got a glimpse of the man?"

"Yes, fortunately. Mack was in the breaker shed, trying to fix the power. It's out front, past the end of the drive. He looked up, and caught a glimpse of a tall, muscular fellow with black hair, dressed in dark clothing. He only saw him through the fountain, unfortunately, so while he was able to get an approximate size and shape, the water blurred the face. The evening light couldn't have helped much, either. He went after the chap, but couldn't catch him. The police were encouraged that the man had been seen, at least. Seemed to think it improved chances of recovering our stuff."

"Was it all in the room on the other side of that window?" Miss Miller pointed to the broken frame.

"Heavens, no. My bag was in there, and Aldred's medal case. The Holberts' things were with their coats in the foyer. That's where the clock was, too. The swan was in the hallway between the reception room and the foyer."

"It was a reasonably audacious burglary, then."

Nella frowned. "I suppose so. I confess to feeling quite strenuous exasperation towards the culprit rather than admiration, however."

"No, quite so," Miss Miller said. "I'm just trying to build a picture of the whole thing. Where did you say that the butler was?"

"I'm not sure I did. Lloyd was with us in the dining room initially, and helped Cook bring things through. Then he went back with her to the kitchens. He normally eats at the same time that we do, only back there, obviously. That way he's available if necessary once we've finished dinner."

"But he would have been with your cook in the meantime."

"Indeed."

Miss Miller smiled. "Well then, my dear, in that case it's all perfectly simple."

What does Miss Miller think happened, and why?

HINT

CLARITY

The Sloop Man

Claude Kenton was a celebrated builder of extremely chic, faux 18th-century sloops. Early in his career, he'd constructed one for just the right avid yachtsman, and his business had taken off. A decade later, his constructions were prized countrywide, and there was a four-year waiting list for his services. His murder caused horrified shock among the sailing set, though it delighted the lucky few who already owned one of his creations, as their prized sloops quadrupled in value literally overnight.

The unlucky fellow who'd discovered the corpse was Kenton's childhood friend Watson Hayes. Well known in his own right, Hayes was a sculptor who primarily worked in wood, his statues gracing banks, head offices, well-to-do homes, and even the odd museum or two. Many of Kenton's boats boasted a Watson Hayes figurehead, and undoubtedly each man's work had helped the exposure of the other's.

Josh Cole met Watson Hayes at his workshop. Hayes was a soft-spoken, slender man with long dark hair and unusually intense eyes. Several large chunks of wood stood around the workshop, seemingly untouched. Two others had large sheets of tarpaulin draped over them.

"I don't let anyone see them until they're finished," Hayes said.

Josh jumped slightly. "I beg your pardon?"

"The pieces I'm working on. I saw you staring at the sheets. I don't let anyone see them until they're finished. It puts me off. I don't want other eyes polluting what I can see."

"Ah. My apologies. No pollution intended. My name is—"

"Joshua Cole, yes," said Hayes. "You want to know about Claude."

"That's right," Josh said, becoming slightly wary.

Hayes gestured towards some chairs. "Please, sit." Once they were both settled, he nodded to himself. "Claude was like fire. Energetic, full of passion, sometimes warm and reassuring, sometimes ferocious and frightening. The world is a smaller, colder place without him in it. We met when we were little. Even then, I could see the light burning in him. I was helpless to resist it. Through school, I was his dark shadow. That suited me just fine. I don't always really understand people, and I'm not very comfortable being in the limelight. Claude was a very generous god. Somehow we ended up here. I really don't know what happens next."

"I understand that you found Claude after the attack."

"Yes." Hayes nodded again, his eyes like saucers. "There are some sights that are too terrible to be borne. He was face down next to a hull he had been working on, all swooping lines and taut power. There was a knife between his shoulder blades. It looked obscene, squatting there like a toad on his body."

"Wait," Josh said. "The knife was shaped like a toad?"

"No! What a curious imagination you have, Mr. Cole. You must have seen so many terrible, terrible things. Your poor eyes. The knife was shaped like a knife. Death written in tight, hard edges. I know it was wrong of me, but I couldn't leave Claude lying there on the ground like that. He didn't belong there, in that pool of old blood. He was fire, not earth. So I moved him back inside, to near his desk. He left a long smear of blood, all the way back into his warehouse. There was no help for it. He needed to be near his things. Without its things, fire can't exist. There was no fire left, though. His skin was pale and waxy. All the heat had already fled, leeched into the air and the ground. That was the moment when I truly understood death."

"Oh?"

"Death is entropy, Mr. Cole. The dissipation of everything that you are, all your elemental energy, dissolving into an infinite cloud of identical, indistinguishable nothingness. Without differentiation, how would you tell a log from a girl's eyes? That's what death is. But I can see you understand. You're water." He paused. "You'd have hated Claude."

"On that note, did Claude have any enemies?"

"Enemy is such a strange word, don't you think? To hate someone so strongly that you think about them always, set your life against theirs, bend to them, work around them—what is that but love, reflected? I don't think Claude had any enemies, no. There was a rival who found Claude offensive, a man named Filipe who had built pretty boats before Claude did, a man who did not succeed. But I would hesitate to use the word 'enemy', I think."

"Can you tell me anything more about Filipe?"

"No. I can not. I know nothing more. In my mind, he too is water."

"Right. Well, thanks for your time, Mr. Hayes. It's been very interesting."

Back at the office, Josh put a call through to Pete at the police department. "Kenton, the dead boat builder," he said. "I'm pretty certain that his sculptor friend killed him."

Why does Josh suspect Watson Hayes?

HINTS

BLOOD

The Insurance Salesman

Inspector Parnacki looked around the dead man's office. It was meticulously tidy, and generously sized, with anodyne art on the walls. As well as a desk with comfortable-looking office chairs both in front of and behind it, there was a sofa along one wall, with a coffee table in front of it. Any paperwork had been put away.

The victim, who'd been found on the sofa, was named Arden Simms. He sold business insurance for his firm, Holbert's Insurance, and apparently had been highly successful. The rich tan of his skin was contrasted by the pale band where he wore his wedding ring, and suggested that he'd recently been on a vacation. He'd been shot repeatedly in the chest and torso, but the gun was not at the scene. Parnacki went to contact the man's next of kin, leaving his colleagues to gather evidence and canvass local residents.

The next morning, preliminary reports on Simms's murder were available. The gunshots had been reported at 7.45pm by a cleaner who had heard them from a nearby building. Unfortunately she had not seen anything useful, and canvassing had not turned up any witnesses. Simms and his wife Donna lived in a reasonably prosperous area of the city and did not have any children. Evidence in Simms's effects indicated a mistress, and the man's assistant, Christian Barnett, had reluctantly identified the woman as one Ebba Ganton. Inspector Parnacki decided to start by interviewing his widow.

Even in the depths of grief and shock, Donna Simms came across as a friendly, pleasant woman. She was in her early thirties, with auburn hair. Inspector Parnacki offered her a cup of coffee, and thanked her for coming in.

"Actually, getting out the house is a blessed relief," she said. "I should be thanking you. How can I help?"

"I'm just trying to gather a picture of your husband's life recently," said the inspector.

"Oh, that's easy. Work. Arden was a total workaholic. He was at the office until gone ten at least three nights a week. Sometimes he had to go in at the weekend, too. I knew that about him all along, of course. Clients don't really care about

your schedule. I'd hoped that maybe the hours would slacken off a little over the years, but no, it was every bit as bad as ever. I was amazed that I finally managed to get him to come on vacation this year."

"You went away?"

"Yes, we had two weeks in a lovely little beach resort on the coast. The weather was perfect. Arden even managed to relax." Her face crumpled, and she started crying. The inspector passed her a box of tissues, and she dabbed her eyes. "I suppose it was a nice way to say goodbye. We only got back five days ago. I used to joke that working so much would kill him, but I never thought his death would be at the hands of some burglar."

"Did your husband have any . . . outside interests, do you know?"

She laughed bitterly. "What, you mean like sport, or drinking? Or another woman? Hardly. Holbert's barely left him enough time for the life he had. He was always tired. Poor Arden. Now, at last he'll get to properly rest."

A couple of hours after Donna Simms had left, Ebba Ganton arrived for her interview. She was younger and prettier than Donna, with none of the other woman's friendliness. However, the grief and shock were just as evident on her face.

"Tell me about Arden Simms," Inspector Parnacki said to her.

"He was lovely. We've been together for a couple of years now. He worked far too much, though. If his mother had been less of a burden, he might have had more time. I was going to marry him. I had it all worked out. I thought he might ask me a couple of days ago, on his return from a trip somewhere, but he didn't. Now he never will."

"So you didn't know he was married?"

"What? Impossible."

He passed her a copy of the Simms's marriage certificate.

The blood drained from her face. "I . . . see," she said, quietly. Tears welled in her eyes. "And his mother?"

"Dead for almost a decade, I believe."

She stood up, slightly unsteadily. "I have to go."

Inspector Parnacki stood up as well. "You may of course leave, Miss Ganton, but I'm afraid I'll have to ask you to remain in the city. You might wish to retain the services of a defence lawyer. I will have a considerable number of further questions."

Why does Inspector Parnacki suspect Ebba Ganton?

HINTS
MOTIVES

The Boxton Liquor Store

oxton Liquor was an unprepossessing store in one of the city's poorer quarters. The windows were sealed over with permanent metal grilles, the door was similarly reinforced, and even the little service window at the far end of the main fronting looked as if it could withstand a modest cavalry assault. A tatty piece of card inside the window by the door indicated that it locked at 6pm, when service switched to window only. A metal sign advertising a leading brand of beer tottered

drunkenly in front of it, glinting in the afternoon light. Gaudy green awnings kept the rain off the windows, but did nothing to keep the metal grilles from rusting. Cigarette butts littered the pavement around the door.

"Charming," Josh Cole said.

Adam Matthews, his photographer, just grunted.

"Want to get any images of the outside of the place?"

"Definitely not."

When Pete, Josh's police contact, had told him about the plucky cashier who'd almost been killed by a lunatic the night before, he'd promised that the story would be photogenic, so long as he went there after midday today. Josh sighed.

"I reckon all those doughnuts are addling your buddy's brain," Adam said.

"Well, we're here. Let's go on in."

They went into the shop, and a tall, muscular young man looked round. Suddenly, Josh understood. The lad was so handsome as to be almost pretty, with jet black hair and piercing green eyes. He had a nasty dark bruise at the top of his nose, which somehow accented his looks rather than marring them.

"Guess it wasn't the doughnuts after all," Adam muttered.

"Hey there," Josh said pleasantly. "I'm Josh Cole, from the *Sentinel*. We heard you had quite the heroic adventure last night. Could be front-page news. Can you answer a few questions?"

The lad grinned, lighting his face up. "Alex Dunlap. It'd be a real pleasure, Mr. Cole."

While Adam set up his camera and started taking photos, Josh got Dunlap to talk him through the events of the previous night.

"It was about nine. I remember the time because I was working six to midnight, and I was glad to be halfway through my shift. This guy came into the store while I was sweeping. At first, I didn't really think much of it. He was tall, taller than me, with very short, very blond hair, and really pale blue eyes. He was wearing a long, heavy black coat. He came up to the counter, so I asked if I could help. He told me 'Yes, you can give me your money,' and pulled a gun. There was an anchor tattooed on the back of his hand, and he had a strong accent, kinda like German or Dutch, but flatter and harder. You know?"

Josh nodded. "Scandinavian, maybe."

"I guess? I was really shocked, so I just stared at him. Then he leant forward, and smashed his forehead hard between my eyes. I fell back, landed in the rum and gin, and went sprawling. I was out cold for a bit. When I came round, I was tied up. The guy was going through the register, emptying it. I started to say something, and he turned around, and tapped the gun barrel across his lips. I know when to shut up, so I did. He started to leave, and I thought maybe that was it, but it wasn't. There was a bunch of promotional leaflets on the counter. He pulled out a lighter, lit it, winked at me, and tossed it on the leaflets. Then he left."

Josh looked at the counter. It had been recently scrubbed, but there were still scorch marks visible. "Huh."

Alex nodded. "Yeah. I tried to get up, but I was trussed like a turkey. Lucky for me, when I was a kid, I busted my shoulder up.

Since then, I've been able to pop it out. It hurts, but hell, well worth it. I smacked it out of joint on the floor, and fought my way out of the ropes. The whole counter was starting to catch, so I high-tailed it over to the club soda, and started pouring it over the counter. If I hadn't been able to weasel out of the ropes like that, I'd be a tragic fire accident this morning. I guess he didn't want to risk a gunshot attracting attention."

"Wow," Josh said. "That's quite a story. I'm amazed you're at work today."

"Mr. Shultz relies on me," Alex said proudly.

When Adam had taken all the photos he needed, and they were walking away from the shop, Josh sighed heavily. "That kid really needs to work on his stories, and keep his fingers out of the till."

Why does Josh think Alex is lying?

HINT

PRACTICALITY

The Gales

fter a young woman's body was discovered in Crowford Park early on Saturday morning, Inspector Parnacki was at the scene within forty-five minutes. He arrived at the park to see a sizeable police operation already set up, and was directed towards a section of path through the park which had been ringed with investigation tape. He spotted a technician whom he knew, a man in his forties named Darrell Chastain, and went over to him.

"Inspector," Chastain said, and nodded a greeting.

"Darrell. What do we know?"

"The victim was Thelma Terry, seventeen years old. Lives over on Bryce Street, from her purse. An officer has gone to tell the parents. She's been dead since last night. Can't be much more precise, given the exposure. One stab wound, to the back. A nasty one. The weapon is missing, but it could have been a hunting knife. From the blood, I'd say she was stabbed about 10 feet back up the path. She fell down, it looks like, then got back up and managed a few steps. No suggestion of any fight, restraint, or assault, just the knife-wound. That's it, so far."

"Thank you," Parnacki said. "I'll let you get on with it. Tell me if you get anything more."

The girl was dressed casually, with long, heavy skirts, sturdy shoes, and a shawl and cardigan over a thick blouse. Sensible clothing, given the weather. He paced back along the path to where the initial attack had taken place. No sign of struggle. Just a lot of blood. Smeared footsteps and fat, round droplets tracked her movements up to her final location. It would have been quick, at least.

The section of path where it had happened was quite exposed, away from trees and shrubs. A lamp-post was nearby, but as he got close to it, he could clearly see that its housing and mechanism were shattered, the interior weathered by several weeks of exposure. His imagination showed him the girl walking into darkness, and not emerging. There were several officers searching the grounds of the park, both nearby and further afield, looking for the knife. He decided to leave them to it.

When he got back to the station, the girl's parents were waiting for him. Sam and Bernice Terry were in their late thirties, dressed in moderately prosperous clothing with the sort of unconscious similarity of style that often comes with long relationships. Beneath the obvious shock and grief, the pale skin and tear-stained cheeks, they looked pleasant, mild people.

"I'm so sorry for your loss," he told them, perfectly sincerely. "Thank you for coming here. My name is Inspector Parnacki, and I'll be doing everything I can to locate the person who did this and arrest them. I need to know anything you can tell me about Thelma's movements yesterday."

Sam Terry nodded, visibly steeling himself. His wife gripped his hand. "Thel went to visit her cousin yesterday, after lunch. Ewan is my brother's boy. His mother, Alene, died a few years ago, and Vic, my brother, he withdrew into himself. Thel started going round there regularly after that, trying to give Ewan a sort of big sister, I guess. They live the other side of the park. She said to expect her back around 7.30pm, but the gales were terrible yesterday evening, so when she didn't turn up, we figured she'd decided to give them a chance to die down. When it got to 9pm, and the wind was still going, I assumed she'd just stay over there. She's done it before in bad weather. Otherwise she always comes straight back. Always. It was almost ten before the wind eased. When your man knocked, I thought it was . . ." He dissolved into quiet, racking sobs. His wife clutched at him, crying as well.

The inspector turned away from them to look out of the window, giving them a modicum of privacy. The next port of call would clearly have to be the uncle. Eventually the Terrys gathered themselves a little, and he turned back round to them.

"May I trouble you for your brother's address, Mr. Terry?" Parnacki asked. "We'll need to talk to him to find out exactly what happened."

"Of course," Sam said automatically. He scribbled an address down on a notepad.

"Thank you," the inspector said. As Sam began to open his mouth, Parnacki added, "We'll find her murderer, Mr. Terry, and you will be informed once the culprit is in custody."

Sam nodded, and he and his wife left.

Victor Terry's house had a shabby air to it. The external paint was dirty and peeling in places, the front garden was somewhat unkempt and played host to a few old, discarded toys, and the small fence that divided the property from the pavement needed a bit of repair. The other properties on the street were picture-perfect, and the comparison was not kind. Inspector Parnacki went up to the front door, and knocked. The man who answered looked like he belonged in the house—his hair was a bit too long, his clothes were old and wearing out, and his posture suggested boredom. His eyes were as hard as gimlets, however. It was rather as if Sam Terry had been put through five years of hard drinking in rough bars.

"Victor Terry?" the inspector asked. "My name is Inspector Parnacki. May I talk with you inside for a moment?"

Victor's eyes narrowed slightly. "What's this about?"

"I'd rather not discuss the matter on your doorstep."

"All right then," the man said, after a long hesitation. He turned and walked back into the house.

Parnacki followed, closing the door behind him, and found himself in a narrow, wood-panelled hallway. Terry led the way into an austere living room. There was a fire in the hearth with a painting of a pretty woman in white hanging above it, and a large black crucifix hung on another wall, but otherwise the room held only heavy furniture and a dark red rug. A casual table with some uncomfortable-looking wooden chairs sat in front of the window. The man pulled out one of those and dropped into it, gesturing at the inspector to take another.

As he did so, a small, shy-looking boy came into the doorway and froze, his eyes like saucers. Parnacki offered him as kindly a smile as he could. Ewan just stared at him.

"Leave us," Victor said.

Ewan dropped his head. "Yes, sir." His voice was a monotonous mumble. He turned, and was gone.

Victor turned back to the inspector.

"What's this about, then?"

"I'm afraid I have bad news,"

Parnacki said. "It's about your niece, Thelma."

The man flinched inwards. "Is she . . . ?"

Parnacki nodded. "I'm afraid she's dead, yes. She was killed last night."

Victor's face paled. He said nothing.

"I understand she was here yesterday, visiting her cousin," said the inspector.

"Yes," the man said, finally. His voice was matter-of-fact. "She arrived around midday, prepared some lunch, and then spent the afternoon with the boy. She left around 7pm, when the boy goes to bed."

"The storm didn't put her off, then?"

"What? The wind? No. It wasn't raining."

"I see," Parnacki said. "Do you know what she and your son did during the afternoon?"

"Boy!" bellowed Victor, making the inspector jump slightly.

Hasty footsteps approached from elsewhere in the house, and then Ewan appeared in the doorway again. He stayed there, as if awaiting permission to enter.

"What did you and your cousin do yesterday?" Victor demanded.

"Played," Ewan said, sounding fearful and confused.

Victor grimaced. "Sweet Lord, grant me strength. Where did you play? What did you play?" His voice sounded harsher than before.

"The park, sir," said Ewan quickly. "We played ball, and looked at birds and flowers, and talked."

"Better. Did you speak to anyone else?"

"The mean boy came, but then he left again. That's all sir, I promise."

Victor nodded, once. "Very well. And she departed when you went to bed, at seven, yes?"

Ewan stared at him, and bobbed nervously. "Yes, sir."

"You won't ever see her again," Victor said flatly. "She's dead, like your mother. Now leave us alone." Suddenly as white as a sheet, Ewan fled, silent tears streaming down his face. "My apologies, Inspector. The boy is soft. He has always been soft."

Inspector Parnacki made a safely anonymous noise, forcing his face into neutrality. "He mentioned a mean boy."

"Douggie Norman. The local bully. Lives the next street over, towards the park. His family's house is called 'Boleskin'. He's pestered my niece before."

"Thank you. I should go and speak with this young man directly." He stood up. "My thanks for your time."

Victor nodded. "You can see yourself out, I'm sure."

Parnacki left the house with a certain relief, and made his way to Douggie Norman's home. It was of a very similar design to Victor Terry's, but rigorously neat, down to the last painted-over nail. He knocked on the door.

A sour-looking woman opened it, took one glance at the inspector, and frowned. "What's he done now?"

"Mrs. Norman?"

"No, I'm Princess Pocohontas, and you couldn't be more of a policeman if you tried. Douggie's not here."

"I see," Inspector Parnacki said. "You get a lot of these visits, then."

"More than my share. He'll be back at nine. I don't know where he goes or what he's doing. Don't want to know, neither. Given up trying to control him, me and Bruce have. But he knows that if he wants to call this place home, he's to be in by nine, and to stay in until seven in the morning. He's many things, my Douglas, but he's not stupid enough to cross his old mother." She folded her arms and glared at the inspector. "Not many are."

"And he was here last night?"

"Are you deaf? Yes, he was here last night. He got in at a minute to nine, all wind-blown. I went to bed at 10.30, but him and Bruce were up until well past midnight, talking about the dogs."

"Thank you, Mrs. Norman," the inspector said. "I'll be sure to call after 9pm if I need to speak to your son."

She eyed him up and down. "You do that. Good day, officer."

Parnacki walked back to the pavement, clenched his hand into a fist, and allowed himself a satisfied smirk. "Gotcha," he said.

What happened to Thelma Terry?

HINTS

A) WEATHER CONDITIONS PROVED RELEVANT TO THE CASE.

B) THELMA'S MURDER WAS PERSONAL, NOT RANDOM.

C) POLICE EVENTUALLY FOUND THE MURDER WEAPON BURIED HASTILY IN A FLOWER-BED IN THE PARK.

D) EWAN TERRY WOULD GO ON TO BECOME A REASONABLY WELL-RESPECTED PAINTER.

E) ALENE TERRY'S DEATH WAS RULED A SUICIDE.

F) SAM AND VICTOR HAD BEEN RAISED BY ALCOHOLIC PARENTS. THEY WERE NOT ESPECIALLY CLOSE.

The Star of Rajpur

iss Miller had first met Emmeline Peterson at finishing school. Being from similar backgrounds, and both possessed of a certain kind of wry humour, they quickly became friends. Although their paths through life had diverged after entering adulthood, the two ladies remained close. So when Emmeline's husband Bennett presented her with the Star of Rajpur, a large, deep blue sapphire with a legendary history, Miss Miller was the first to know. When Emmeline decided to have the Star set into a lavish necklace, Miss Miller was the first to know. And when Emmeline discovered that the Star had been stolen, Miss Miller was once again the first to know—after the police and the insurers, of course.

That afternoon saw the two ladies taking tea in the reception room of Emmeline's home. Miss Miller was glad to see that her friend was infuriated by the theft, rather than despondent.

"The timing is very suspicious, of course," Emmeline said. "I got the finished piece back from Rimel's yesterday lunchtime. By ten last night, it was just a bent mass of empty sockets. Poor Mr. Rimel was devastated. He was so delighted at the chance to set the Star."

"They didn't take the gold?"

"No. Damnedest thing. I had Mr. Rimel surround the Star with a triple ring of paste gems, increasingly light shades of blue. I wanted to set the Star off, but it seemed rude to try to compete with it, if you see what I mean. Anyway, they were all prised clumsily out of the setting. The paste pieces are pretty enough, but they're totally worthless. It must have taken several minutes to get them out. I can't imagine why they bothered." She gestured to a lacquered box on the table. "The setting is in there, if you want a look. The police have poked at it, and then had it photographed, and I'm sure the insurance chap will want to see as well, so you might as well."

"Maybe I will have a peek," Miss Miller said. She reached across and opened the box. The setting had clearly once been an attractive web of tight gold filigree, shaped like a heart, and with a recurring floral motif in the detail. It clearly didn't weigh a colossal amount, but even so, there was enough there that melted down, it would have paid a modest month's rent. Certainly nothing to sneeze at. She closed the box again. "Odd."

"Isn't it." Emmeline sighed. "The thing that's really got me hopping mad of course is that I'm fairly certain that it wasn't an intruder. Mr. Rimel was the only person who called yesterday, and it's not as if the drive provides much in the way of a hiding place at this time of year. I suppose it's not utterly impossible that some opportunistic sneak-thief crept in through the orchard or the rose gardens, but how would they know? No, I fear it's one of the staff. Knowing that one of the people in your very home has betrayed you like that . . . Horrible. Makes my blood boil!"

"One or more."

"Mary! What a thing to say."

"Oh, sorry my dear. Just thinking aloud."

"You, Miss Miller, have a very devious mind."

"Thank you," she replied, with a bright smile.

"I suppose this means you'll want to interrogate everyone, then." Emmeline pulled a face, pretending distress.

"Rather."

There was a knock at the door, and Collins, the butler, entered the room. He was a professionally dour man who worked hard to suppress his natural sense of fun when he was on duty. He was dressed impeccably, as always. "Madam, the police."

"Very good, Collins," Emmeline said.

A moment later, a young, nervous-looking police officer entered the room. "We've found most of your jewels, Mrs. Peterson."

"Oh?" She arched an eyebrow.

"They were in the undergrowth outside your gate, in a little heap. Forty-eight of them, in different shades of blue. They'll be going in as evidence, of course."

"Am I to assume that the Star was not among them?"

The officer nodded mournfully. "The big, smooth one? No. Sorry."

"Cabochon," said Emmeline.

The officer stared at her.

"Officer," Miss Miller said, breaking the uncomfortable

silence. "Can you tell how long the gems had been out there?"

"Probably overnight," he said gratefully. "There were some leaves and stuff on them, more than you'd see from just a nice day like today."

"Thank you for telling me about the discovery, officer," Emmeline said. "I won't keep you."

"Ma'am," the officer said.

Collins ushered him back out of the room. Less than a minute later, he returned. "There was something else you wanted, Madam." It wasn't a question.

"Yes. Would you indulge Miss Miller by answering a few questions for her about yesterday?"

His expression didn't even waver. "Of course, Madam."

Miss Miller smiled at the butler, just for the sake of it. "Could you talk me through your day yesterday, from the Star's arrival to the discovery of its absence?"

"Yes, ma'am. Mr. Henri Rimel of Rimel's Fine Jewellery arrived shortly before 1pm yesterday afternoon, and left around ten minutes later. Afterwards, I served champagne cocktails to Mr. and Mrs. Bennett, and oversaw luncheon, first for family, then for staff. Effie—the maid—was visiting her parents yesterday, so after my own luncheon, I starched and ironed Mr. Bennett's shirts. Brutus, one of the dogs, required some minor medical attention, so at approximately 3.25pm, I conveyed him to the veterinarian, returning a little before 6pm. I am happy to report that Brutus's claw was successfully dealt with. Most evenings this past month, I have been training Mrs. Brookshire's new girl,

Acie, on the non-culinary elements of her job. Yesterday, we were working again on advanced napkin folds. Dinner for family is served at 7pm, and staff at 8pm. After that was cleaned away, I escorted Mrs. Brookshire to the bus stop, returning a little short of 9.20pm and locking the main gate as I did so. I then assisted Mr. Bennett with some filing, and I was going around the house ensuring windows were closed when Mrs. Bennett raised the alarm regarding her gemstone, which was at 10.05pm."

Miss Miller stared at him. "That was very precise, Collins," she said finally.

"Thank you, ma'am. I try."

"Please ask Mrs. Brookshire to come to us next, Collins," Emmeline said.

"Yes, Madam," he replied. He bowed shallowly, and swept out.

"Is he—" began Miss Miller.

"Oh yes," replied Emmeline. "Always. If Collins has turned against us, I have little doubt that Bennett will be working for him rather than vice versa by this time tomorrow. Bennett did actually offer him a job at the office once, you know. Collins replied that he much preferred looking after people to looking after money."

"A good man," Miss Miller said.

"I do hope so."

A short while later, the cook arrived. Hildegarde Brookshire was as formidable as her name—tall and strong, with a no-nonsense manner. "The girl and I were in the kitchens yesterday," she said, somewhat suspiciously. "Where else would we be?

Cooking, as usual, and cleaning after. Yesterday lunchtime was shepherd's pie, that's easy enough, but the day's bread always takes time, and there was a sponge cake to prepare, then the afternoon was making mushroom soup, and some jam, and pastry for the lamb en croute. Mr. Collins took the girl away for an hour before dinner, so I made sure all the vegetables were sliced, and then she was back in time to help me serve. After we'd eaten as well, Mr. Collins walked me to the bus. All perfectly normal."

Mrs. Brookshire's assistant, Acie Justin, was a thin, nervous young woman who seemed to be forever on the edge of dropping a curtsey. She was clearly unsettled by Miss Miller's questions. "I don't rightly know what to say, ma'am. It was a normal afternoon. I helped Cook with the baking, washed the crockery and pots, polished the tableware, set the table, mopped the floors, tended some hearths, and all that. I was with her all day, apart from my hour with Mr. Collins, who's teaching me napkins at the moment. When Cook left after dinner, I finished the washing up and cleaned the floors and surfaces. I'm in the room next to Effie's, who was at her Dad's yesterday, but I stay in the kitchens until everybody goes to bed in case someone needs a mug of a tea or something."

Last up were the groundsman Sidney Cutshaw, and his assistant, a teenage lad named Brady. Collins delivered them unshod, and withdrew. Mr. Cutshaw was a short man in late middle age, with a face that looked like it had been carved from oak, and a rather spectacular moustache. His assistant was tall and brawny, clearly overawed, and, so far as Miss Miller could discern, not very bright.

"Yesterday lunchtime, I was trimming hedges near the rose garden. Young Brady here was raking leaves and twigs off the drive."

"I was," Brady said. "I saw that man arrive." He frowned. "I thought he was nice, but he wasn't. He was nasty."

"Brady!" Mr. Cutshaw said. "Don't talk like that." He turned back to Emmeline. "Sorry, ma'am."

"It's quite all right," Emmeline said. "I expect Mr. Rimel was rather brusque."

Mr. Cutshaw glowered at his assistant for a moment. "After lunch, I spent several hours mowing the lawns. Brady went to collect a box of seedlings from the nursery that I've been waiting for."

Brady reached into a pocket and proudly fished out a note. "Mr. Cutshaw gave me this to show them."

The groundsman sighed, and nodded. "Lad would forget his own head if he didn't have a note reminding him not to leave it behind. Anyway, I finished the mowing by six. Brady was back by then, so we raked up the cut grass."

"Then I went to fetch the logs," Brady said. "Like I always do."

"The wood bin is up by the gate," Cutshaw explained. "The lad fetches firewood morning and evening."

"So you were both around the grounds all day," Miss Miller said. "Did either of you see anyone enter or leave?"

"Just Mr. Collins, with one of the dogs," Cutshaw said. "He was out for a little more than two hours."

"And the nasty man," Brady said.

"Don't call him that, boy," Cutshaw said.

Brady bobbed his head unhappily. "Sorry ma'ams, Mr. Cutshaw. Won't happen again."

"We turn in at nine-thirty," said the groundsman. "After dinner's had a chance to settle. That's all there is to tell."

Miss Miller nodded.

Once Collins had brought another pot of tea and left the ladies in peace, Miss Miller turned to her friend. "What about you and Bennett? What were your movements? Did you see anything?"

"Not a thing," Emmeline said. "Bennett went off shooting in the orchard in the afternoon. I was in the drawing room, reading a rather dull book. I could see Mr. Cutshaw going back and forth across the lawns with the mower. I'm afraid I rather dozed off. Bennett got back with his dogs shortly after six, since the light was failing. The commotion woke me up. We chatted for a while, then had dinner, and digestifs in the drawing room. I read for a bit more, and decided to have one further look at Rimel's work before bed."

"And where was the Star?"

"It's been in here all day, actually. It never occurred to me that I might need to immediately lock it in the safe."

"Ah," Miss Miller said. "In that case, I may have an idea of where the stone is."

What happened to the Star of Rajpur?

HINTS

A) EFFIE WEBSTER REALLY WAS ACROSS TOWN ALL DAY WITH HER PARENTS.

B) COLLINS RATHER DISAPPROVES OF BANKING.

C) MR. RIMEL WAS SURPRISINGLY UNPLEASANT TO BRADY, AND CONSIDERS THE YOUNG MAN AN OUTRIGHT IDIOT.

D) MRS. BROOKSHIRE TAKES LEFT-OVER FOOD FROM DINNER HOME TO HER FAMILY. MRS. PETERSON KNOWS, AND DOESN'T MIND.

E) ACIE JUSTIN IS QUITE AMBITIOUS, AND MADE OF STERNER STUFF THAN SHE APPEARS TO BE.

F) MR. CUTSHAW DOESN'T MUCH CARE FOR THE PETERSONS, BUT HE DOES GENUINELY LOVE THEIR GROUNDS.

G) BRADY IVEY WOULDN'T KNOW A SAPPHIRE IF YOU

THREW IT AT HIM.

H) SHOOTING IS BENNETT PETERSON'S FAVOURITE PURSUIT BY FAR.

I) EMMELINE PETERSON GREATLY PREFERS TO HAVE READ A FASHIONABLE BOOK THAN TO ACTUALLY BE IN THE PROCESS OF READING IT.

J) NO ONE LIED TO MISS MILLER.

K) TAKING ALL THE STONES WAS RISKY AND INEFFICIENT.

The Birdwatcher

Miss Miller had come to Mike Rathbone's party with few expectations. Mike was a keen member of the city's birdwatching circles, but she knew little about him outside that arena. She arrived to find that he and his wife Lorraine lived in a very pleasant little four-bedroom house in a quiet area. The garden was generous, and bird-feeders hung from at least half a dozen different trees. Several other birders were in attendance, including Alison Householder, a pleasant woman whom Miss Miller hadn't seen for several months. The pair of them were chatting together in the drawing room when a horrible shriek from upstairs silenced the entire room. A woman's voice called for help, and the entire gathering surged out of the room and upstairs.

On the landing, outside the bathroom, Rebecca Hood was kneeling on the floor and crying over her husband Martin, who was unconscious and bleeding from a nasty-looking gash on the back of his head. Everyone crowded around, aghast. His breathing looked reasonably strong, and his clothing was undisturbed, but he obviously needed immediate medical attention.

"Rebecca," Miss Miller said sharply. The woman jerked wildly upright. A table behind her wobbled, and a vase fell to the floor with an unhealthy crack. "We need to get him to hospital right now."

She blinked. "Yes, of course. Hospital."

The two strongest-looking men at the party were Mike, and

Willis McGee, whose wife Gertie was one of the circle. Miss Miller pointed at the two men. "Gentlemen, get him downstairs and into a car, and then get moving. Mine will do if necessary."

"I'll take him," Rebecca said immediately. She looked around the group warily. "We have a car. I'm not leaving him for an instant."

"Fair enough," Mike said. "Willis, let's get Martin out of here."

"*Gently*," Miss Miller said. "As gently as you can."

The men lifted Martin carefully, and slowly made their way downstairs. Rebecca was right on their heels, and the rest of the group followed on behind. Miss Miller listened carefully, but all she could make out were the group on the stairs, Rebecca's sniffling, someone coughing, a latch closing, and Martin's ragged breaths.

A few minutes later, Rebecca had left with Martin, and the party reassembled in the drawing room. Miss Miller quickly counted heads. Everyone was present and correct—Mike and Lorraine Rathbone, Zettie and David Moses, Willis and Gertie McGee, Alison Householder, and Tillman Symes.

"I'm going to check upstairs," Mike declared. "Make sure he's not hiding somewhere."

"Take someone with you," Miss Miller said quickly.

"I'll go," Willis said.

David Moses nodded. "Tillman and I will have a look down here."

The two pairs headed off to ensure the house was free of intruders.

"Well, ladies," Miss Miller said. "Which of you know Martin Hood properly?"

"I know him to chat to," Zettie Moses said.

"As do I," said Alison.

Gertie and Lorraine shook their heads.

Miss Miller nodded. "So. Have either of you spoken to him recently?"

"What is this all about, Mary?" asked Alison.

"Someone must have bashed the poor fellow over the head," Miss Miller said. "If it was just some random robber who happened to sneak in while we were chatting, why didn't he at least take Martin's pocket watch and search for a wallet? It's not as if we knew what had happened until Rebecca screamed. I don't recall seeing Martin for a good five minutes beforehand. There was plenty of time for someone bold enough to break into a party to also rifle through an unconscious man's pockets. So maybe it was personal?"

Lorraine gasped, her eyes wide. Alison went pale.

"I saw him a couple of days ago," Zettie said slowly. "I bumped into him in the old deer park. He seemed fine. Perfectly cheerful. He works in rural property sales, and said that business had been steady. We discussed a place he'd put on the books earlier in the week, an old farm near a small river to the west of the city. He'd spotted kingfishers, and was planning to go back on Sunday to really spend some time out there, using business as a good excuse.

He didn't appear to be worried about anything in particular. He asked after David, I asked after Rebecca. That was about it."

"That's more recent than me," Alison said. "I bumped into him a couple of weeks ago at an auction. We exchanged pleasantries, that's about it. If there was anything bothering him, he hid it well enough. I was hardly interested in prying into any dark secrets he might have, though."

Gertie shrugged. "I had a reasonable chat with him earlier this evening. The usual small-talk. He didn't appear to be concerned that some mystery assailant would suddenly leap out and attack him."

"This is just horrible," Lorraine said. "I can't imagine it. Some blackguard breaking into my home and attacking poor Martin!" She shuddered. "What if he comes back?"

"That's very unlikely," Miss Miller said, her voice soothing. "It's most uncommon for thieving villains to come back for a second attempt—and if he is after Martin, there would be no reason to come back here, would there?"

"I suppose not." Lorraine folded her arms tightly.

Mike and Willis came back into the drawing room, looking slightly dusty. "No sign of anything out of place," Mike said. "We looked in all the cupboards, under all the beds, anywhere you might fit a man. Nothing."

"Same here," said David, as he and Tillman returned. "The downstairs area is completely free of intruders. He must have already made his escape."

"Yes," Mike agreed. "The window in one of the small bedrooms was wide open. We keep those windows closed, so he must have let himself out that way. The poker from the room's fire is also lying on the floor, so my suspicion is that he attacked Martin with that."

"Was anything missing from upstairs, Mike?" Miss Miller asked. "And what about a way in?"

"Nothing appeared to be missing, no. I had a look at Lorraine's jewels, of course, and our various nice bits. Unfortunately my father's Russian vase is sporting a nasty crack, but everything's accounted for."

"The intruder probably bumped it when he attacked Martin," David said. "Obviously Tillman and I don't know the contents of the house, but the kitchen window was unlatched. It wasn't open, but it's not a complete stretch to imagine our lad coming in through there, pushing it to behind him, and making his way upstairs to rifle through the place while we were all in the drawing room. Martin must have gone up to use the bathroom and surprised the chap, who then hit him, panicked, and fled out through the small bedroom with the open window."

"It's certainly possible," Mike said. "I guess Martin found him before he had time to do anything. I really hope he isn't going to pay too badly for our good fortune."

"Will he be all right?" Zettie asked.

"I expect so," Mike said.

"It's hard to say," Miss Miller put in. "Being knocked out is a surprisingly dangerous thing. Not everyone survives."

"Mary!" Lorraine looked horrified.

"I'm very sorry my dear, but it is the truth."

Tillman nodded. He'd gone quite pale. "A cousin of mine knocked himself out by running into a tree head-first when we were children. I don't remember what he was trying to prove, but it seemed really funny at the time. But he didn't wake up, so we went to get help. He never regained consciousness. We buried him three weeks later."

"I'm sorry for your loss," Miss Miller said. "It must have been terrible."

Tillman nodded again, but said nothing.

"We should all be prepared for a police investigation," Miss Miller said. "Hopefully not a murder investigation, but . . . I suggest that everyone gives some thought to their experiences of the evening, and attempts to fix them in their minds before discussing them any further. When the police become involved, they'll be quite grateful for accurate remembered details." She cast her eye over the group. Tillman and Mike looked grim. David, Lorraine, Alison and Zettie were all pale. Gertie and Willis were sharing a wary glance. "Lorraine, my dear, why don't I give you a hand preparing a round of drinks? I think we could all use something to steady our nerves."

Lorraine nodded silently. Miss Miller put an arm around her shoulders and steered her towards the kitchen. Once they were out of the room, she said, "You must be strong, dear. I'm going to find a policeman. Tell them I've gone to powder my nose or something, but make absolutely sure no one leaves. There's no way to tell yet if it was attempted or successful murder, but the culprit is in the drawing room. Say nothing, and you will all be perfectly safe."

Who does Miss Miller suspect of the attack, and why?

HINTS

A) MIKE RATHBONE WAS HUGELY EMBARRASSED BY SOMEONE COMING TO HARM AT A PARTY HE HAD ORGANIZED, AND FELT IT WAS A VAST PERSONAL SLIGHT.

B) LORRAINE RATHBONE HAD NOT MET MARTIN BEFORE THE PARTY.

C) MARTIN HOOD ONLY STAYED IN THE CITY BECAUSE REBECCA FOUND THE COUNTRYSIDE DULL AND STIFLING.

D) REBECCA RESENTED HER HUSBAND'S FASCINATION WITH THE GREAT OUTDOORS.

E) DAVID MOSES NEVER REALLY GOT OVER LOSING HIS FIRST LOVE, ADELE, WHO WALKED OUT ON HIM ONE AFTERNOON WITH NO EXPLANATION.

F) ZETTIE MOSES ALWAYS HAD BEEN OUTGOING AND CHIRPY, BUT WAS FINDING IT AN INCREASING EFFORT.

G) WILLIS McGEE LOST A SIGNIFICANT AMOUNT OF MONEY ON A LAND DEAL OF MARTIN'S.

H) GERTIE McGEE THOUGHT MARTIN WAS A FOOL.

I) ALISON HOUSEHOLDER HAD BEEN ACTIVELY AVOIDING MISS MILLER.

J) TILLMAN SYMES WAS A SHY MAN WHO FELT MOST AT EASE WITH BOOKS.

The Double Widow

Camilla McMurray was every journalist's dream woman—beautiful, glamorous, and tragic, with a hint of scandal. Despite being only twenty-eight, she'd just been widowed for the second time, and violently to boot. Consequently, Josh Cole was under orders to get the most dramatic story that he could. Before gathering up his photographer and heading out, Josh had a look over the basics of the story as indicated by the initial reports from his police contact, Pete.

Delmar McMurray, the deceased, had been sixty-two. His father had made a fortune manufacturing a popular syrup, and Delmar had proved a reliable successor. The company remained strong and profitable, and the McMurray family wealth was considerable. Now that he was dead, control of the company had passed to his younger brother, Verner—a significant responsibility which brought little in the way of increased fortune.

Camilla, Delmar's wife, was the primary beneficiary of his non-business assets. She had been widowed previously, at the age of twenty-five. Her first husband had, like Delmar, been a wealthy older industrialist, Floyd Wright. The Wright marriage had lasted four years, ending when the man suffered a fatal heart attack at the age of sixty-four. At the time, the death had not been considered suspicious, but it had left Camilla with a lot of money. Now, after two-and-a-half years of marriage to Delmar, she had gone from merely rich to extremely rich.

The cause of Delmar's death was not under any dispute. He had been in the main bedroom of their house when he was attacked and, after a short scuffle, his throat was cut. An intruder was caught on the grounds and arrested, but denied everything except trespassing, and had walled himself away behind a lawyer.

The McMurrays' home was very large and exquisitely designed, nestled in lovely landscaped grounds designed to show it to maximum advantage. It was completely overshadowed by Camilla herself, who was probably the most beautiful woman that Josh had ever seen. She had deep, intelligent green eyes set in a delicately heart-shaped face that combined sweetness with promise. Her make-up was so artful as to verge on the edge of genius, and her black dress managed to be simultaneously demure and form-fitting. She was even positioned in the room so that a shaft of sunlight fell behind her, lending her a golden glow.

Every instinct of Josh's screamed at him to run, while he still could. Instead, he smiled.

"Thank you for agreeing to talk to the *Sentinel*, Mrs. McMurray. My name is Joshua Cole, and this is my photographer, Adam Matthews.

I'm very sorry for your loss."

She bowed her head sadly. "Thank you, Mr. Cole. It's been terrible."

"Can you imagine any reason why someone would have wanted to harm your husband?" Josh asked. Beside him, Adam set up the camera.

"You mean apart from me? Oh, don't pretend to look shocked, Mr. Cole. It doesn't suit you. I'm neither stupid nor weak, and I'm well aware that—to an outsider—I would appear to have plenty of motive. But it was nothing to do with me. Delmar was a dear, sweet man. An innocent, really. I was very fond of him, much more so than my first husband who, frankly, was something of a mistake. But Delmar was unambitious and reasonable in his business dealings, and honest in his personal ones. There was no room in his life for intrigue. He was neither sufficiently egotistical nor ruthless to make enemies, and none of his relatives benefit substantially from his death. Poor Verner is utterly devastated, both for the loss of his brother and the loss of his day-to-day freedom, but he'll do his duty for McMurray's Condiments. Honestly, I might have believed that it was someone trying to get me imprisoned, except that I'm sure they would have done a better job of it."

"You have enemies?" Josh asked.

"Jealous rivals, perhaps." Her glance demanded that he change the subject.

"If you'll forgive my prying, could you give me an idea of events as you saw them?"

"I was in the bath, which is down the corridor. I heard glass smashing in the bedroom, so I got out, wrapped myself in a large towel, and went to check what had happened." Her voice wavered, and her eyes filled with tears. "Delmar was face down on the floor in a pool of blood. The balcony door, which is glass, was broken, and there were shards all over the balcony. I think I caught a glimpse of a tall, black-clad figure slipping over the edge of the balcony, but it didn't really register with me at the time. I knelt by my husband, and searched for a pulse." She paused, swallowed, then continued. "He was dead. I don't know how long I sat there. There was a knock on the door, and I discovered that I was weeping, loudly. Matthew Cutshaw is Delmar's personal assistant and household manager. He came in, saw the situation, then called for the maid to help me, and dashed off. He returned a few minutes later, saying that he'd caught a ruffian skulking around, and had locked him in the garden shed. The police have him now."

"That sounds awful," Josh said, with some feeling.

"Yes."

"You didn't have any visitors or guests that evening?"

"No. We considered going out—we often do—but decided against it in the end."

Swallowing nervously, he steeled himself to push his luck a little. "You described your first husband as a mistake?"

"I was young and foolish," Camilla said, flatly. "Delmar was my second chance. I'll say no more, except that I wasn't with Floyd when he died. He wasn't even in the city."

"Right. What happens now for Mrs. McMurray?"

"I have no idea. I'm barely able to think about the present, let alone the future." She glanced pointedly at the door. "I am getting weary."

Josh rose swiftly, and nodded to Adam, who had already packed away his apparatus again. "Thank you so much for your time and indulgence. I do have one last question. Do you think I might speak to Mr. Cutshaw?"

"If he wants to talk to you, I have no objections."

"Thank you again," Josh said.

Outside, in the hallway, they found a maid waiting patiently for them to emerge. She readily agreed to show them to Matthew Cutshaw. Josh sent Adam out to photograph the front of the building, and then followed her down the corridor.

"What's your name?" Josh asked her.

"Yetta Shropshire, sir."

"Did you hear anything last night?"

Her shoulders tensed, and she hesitated.

Josh gave her a reassuring smile. "Mrs. McMurray said I could speak to the staff."

"Oh, very well sir. I didn't mean no impertinence. I heard a crash, sir. I thought maybe Izora had dropped something. A minute or two later, I heard the door, then a little after that, Mr. Cutshaw was shouting for help. I went up to see what I could do, but Mrs. McMurray stopped me from going in to . . . to the bedroom. I brought her a drink, and stayed with her until the police came. This is Mr. Cutshaw's office, sir."

Josh thanked her and went inside.

Cutshaw turned out to be a tall, well-muscled, good-looking man in his early thirties. Like Camilla, he was dressed in expensive, well-fitting black clothing. He looked more like a friendly banker's son than a personal assistant.

"My name is Josh Cole, from the *Sentinel*. I've just been interviewing Mrs McMurray. She said that I could speak to you."

"Fair enough," Cutshaw said. "How can I help you, Mr. Cole?"

"Can you tell me about the events of last night?"

"Certainly. I heard glass breaking from upstairs, and when I got to the bedroom, I discovered Mr. McMurray had been attacked by an assailant who'd broken in from the balcony. As soon as I was sure Mrs. McMurray was unharmed, I called for assistance, and went to look for the assailant. Out in the grounds, I found him attempting to slip away. I apprehended him, tied him up securely, locked him in one of the sheds, and then contacted the police."

"That's awfully daring of you."

"I spent some years in the army, Mr. Cole. It taught me discipline, organization, and self-defence. But I admit that I reacted without really thinking it through. I'm lucky he'd ditched the dagger somewhere when I found him."

"I see. Any idea who he was?"

"None," Cutshaw said. "But he was dressed in black, and had a bag with a rope and some tools in it, which the police took."

"Was Mr. McMurray a good employer?"

"Exemplary. I was lucky to have worked for him these last five years. His death is a senseless loss to everyone who had known him."

"And Mrs. McMurray?"

The man's eyes glowed. "She is truly as beautiful inside as she is outside. I have never heard anyone speak a harsh word against her. She deserves only the very best from life."

"Thank you for talking to me." Josh left the assistant, and, with Adam, returned to the office. It took a little wheedling and inducement, but eventually he was able to persuade Pete to make him a copy of the suspect's initial interview, on the condition that none of it made the newspaper directly. Josh collected it, handed over the inducement plus a decent bonus, and went to a coffee shop near the office to have a look.

The suspect's name was Maxie Miles. He was a small man in

his late forties who'd done several stretches in prison for robbery. "Come off it," the report quoted him as saying. "You know this wasn't me. I'm totally straight nowadays, but even if I wasn't I never harmed a fly. No one ever heard me coming or going, and we both know it. I got a tip to come down to that house last night to see something amazing, and it seemed legit, so I did. I shouldn't have trespassed, but I did, and I'm sorry for that. I expected to see a firework display or something. They're always setting off fireworks in that part of town. I love me some fireworks, I do. Instead, this huge gorilla has grabbed me and he's twisting my arm nearly off. He drags me to some shed, ties me up savagely, and leaves me there. That bag of tools was already in there. Knew his knots, that's for sure. I was still there, trying to wriggle

out, when your boys arrived. That's the truth, that is. I've been very straightforward with you, officer, because I've got nothing to hide, which is why I've waited until now to say this: I want my lawyer."

In with Miles's transcript was a description of the tip he'd referred to. It was apparently scrawled on a piece of scrap paper, and just bore the address of the McMurray residence. There was also a comment which read, "Doesn't look like suspect's handwriting." The word "look" had been underlined.

Josh flicked back over his notes from the day, and suddenly things clicked into place. "I know who the killer is!" he said.

Who does Josh suspect of killing Delmar McMurray, and why?

HINTS

A) CAMILLA McMURRAY WAS NEITHER SURPRISED NOR UPSET BY THE DEATH OF HER FIRST HUSBAND, FLOYD WRIGHT.

B) DELMAR McMURRAY WAS A PLEASANT MAN WHO LOVED HIS WIFE BEYOND MEASURE.

C) THE MURDER WEAPON WAS NEVER RETRIEVED.

D) MAXIE MILES LIED ABOUT TWO THINGS.

E) CAMILLA McMURRAY IS AMBITIOUS AND RESOLUTE.

F) MATTHEW CUTSHAW WOULD HAVE DONE ANYTHING FOR CAMILLA McMURRAY.

G) YETTA SHROPSHIRE WAS THE ONLY PERSON WHO TOLD JOSH THE COMPLETE TRUTH.

H) THE BAG OF TOOLS COMPRISED A LENGTH OF STURDY ROPE, A CROWBAR, A GLASS-CUTTING TOOL, TWO IRON SPIKES, A SMALL FLASK OF OIL, A SET OF BASIC LOCK-PICKS, A TORSION WRENCH, A SMALL METAL SAW, A THIN CHISEL, TWO METAL WEDGES, A DOCTOR'S STETHOSCOPE, AND A MEDIUM-SIZED HAMMER.

The Golden Hind

I t took a reasonable amount of nerve to rob a restaurant while it was still serving the last customers of the evening. The Golden Hind, a high-class French restaurant, was on Tilson Street, in the heart of the city's entertainment district. The thief had assaulted the owner, Murray Blevins, then while he was reeling, snatched the contents of the cash register and exited quickly through the back of the building.

Looking around the restaurant, Inspector Parnacki could easily piece together the man's movements. The cash register was at the drinks counter, which was located near the back of the main restaurant area. The restrooms were along the back wall, just a short distance from the open end of the drinks counter. The large swing doors into the kitchen and service area were in the middle of the back wall. Immediately behind them was a corridor which led left toward the rear entrance of the restaurant and the alley behind, and right to the storerooms and ice room. It would have been easy to come out of the restroom to the cash register, and then exit through the swing doors and along the corridor to the alley exit.

On the other side of the corridor, a large arch opened into the kitchen proper, which held numerous hobs, grills and ovens, as well as metal counters, racks of crockery and cutlery, and cupboards full of assorted supplies. One side wall was taken up with cleaning and drying facilities.

"He had a gun," Murray Blevins said. "I was preparing some change for a customer, so the first thing I knew about it was when he stepped up and cracked me across the temple with the butt of the pistol."

Inspector Parnacki made a sympathetic noise. Blevins certainly had a very nasty bruise on the right side of his head.

"It left me pretty dazed, as you can imagine. He pushed me out of the way, grabbed the cash, and then he was gone."

"Can you describe the man?"

"Like I told your officer, he was wearing an Abe Lincoln mask. All I really remember is that mask, the gun, and the heavy coat. He didn't say anything. Heck, I'm saying 'him', but it could have been a woman under there for all I know. I'm not even really sure how tall he was, because I was doubled over. I'm grateful that he didn't hurt any of the staff, though, or rob the customers. If we had to have an armed robbery, this was about as good as I could have hoped for. I could have done without the clunk on the head, though."

Most of the kitchen staff had gone home by the time the robbery happened. The dishwasher, Barney Davenport, hadn't seen or heard anything. The first he'd known about the incident was when Blevins staggered into the kitchen, bleeding, looking for a cloth. The head chef, Buddy Cross, had seen the man, however.

"It was a busy evening. We'd served a lot of food. I was doing some preparation for tomorrow, getting some stuff on to soak overnight, when I heard the doors bang open. My main work

station is against the back wall, over there."
He pointed at a long stretch of counter
beneath a big mirror. "I like to be able
to keep an easy eye on the comings
and goings. So anyway, like I
said, I heard the door bang,
and someone run through. So I
glanced up, and caught a glimpse
of a guy running off down the
corridor. I was busy and tired, so
I didn't think too much of it at the
time."

"Can you describe the man?"

"I didn't get a good look,
and I didn't see his face,
but he was about average
height, I think, with dark
hair and dark clothing. There
was something written on a
note in his left hand, but I
couldn't tell you what. He
was there, and then he was
gone. A few seconds later,
Murray staggered in with
blood on the side of his
head, and Barney and I
leapt to help him. I wish I

could tell you more, but there's just not much else to it."

"Do you think you'd be able to identify him if you saw him again?"

"Well, I don't really know until I try, I guess. But, uh, probably not. He was only there for a moment, and I was thinking about lentils."

The head waiter, Merle Wheeler, had been working at the restaurant for seven years.

"I was near the front of the restaurant," he told Inspector Parnacki. "I'm afraid I didn't hear or see a thing. We had two tables still occupied, so I was mainly paying attention to them, and ensuring that their bills were ready. But I can tell you one thing for certain. He didn't come through the front door."

"Are you certain?"

"Well, I must allow for the possibility that the man arrived here early in the evening, or maybe even at lunchtime, and then locked himself in a stall in the restroom and waited for several hours. That is not impossible. Nobody reported an occupied stall, but unless they went into the restroom repeatedly, why would they think anything of it? But from seven-thirty, I was on the floor continually. I saw every person who came in, and every person who went out, and there were no people unaccounted for. As I'm sure you can imagine, it's quite important to ensure that customers do not just slip away unnoticed."

"I see," the inspector said. "Is it possible that he gained access through the restroom windows?"

"Only if he was very slender," Wheeler said. "The windows are not large. On balance, I think it unlikely."

The other waiter working at the time was named Baldwin Sweet. He'd been at the Golden Hind for three years. "I did get a quick look at the guy, yes. I should have done something to try to help, and I didn't. I feel terrible about it."

"What happened, precisely?"

"I was in the process of clearing table twelve. I was loaded up with half a dozen plates and bowls, and a bunch of wine and water glasses, so I was mainly thinking about getting it all to the kitchen. I straightened up, glanced over at the drinks bar, and saw this guy bent over the cash register. He looked a bit like Abraham Lincoln, from what I could tell. Then Mr. Blevins, who was next to the guy, made some horrible moaning noise. By the time I looked back, the guy was going through the doors. He had a big, dark coat on, I remember. I wanted to go after him, but I'd have had to drop all the crockery, which would have come out of my pay, and probably scared the devil out of tables nine and fourteen, who were still finishing up. I'm sorry."

Inspector Parnacki smiled at him. "It's probably for the best, Mr. Sweet. The man had a gun. If you'd caught up with him, there's every chance you would have been shot."

Sweet swallowed nervously. "Golly."

When the inspector got back from the restaurant, he discovered that officers had brought in three suspects who had been seen in the area shortly after the time of the robbery, around 10pm.

The first was a tall, burly man named Rubin Wilson. According to the police records, he'd been imprisoned twice previously, once for assault, and once for theft. He was primarily known as a hired thug. He was scowling as he was shown into the interview room. He was wearing denim trousers and a white cotton vest, and took advantage of it to flex his significant muscles at the inspector. He had several visible tattoos, all of a religious nature, including a crude portrait of the Virgin Mary on his left upper arm, a crucifix just below the hollow at the base of his throat, and the word 'Jesus' on the back of his right hand. A crucifix hung around his neck on a thin chain, sitting a little below the tattooed one.

"The Golden Hind? No," he said flatly. "Never been there. Never would. Fancy-schmancy trash. I been past it a coupla times, sure. I'm a regular in Lucy's, which is a street over. I was in there last night, that's what I was doing in the area. Meeting a pal.

Harley Rozella. We were there 'til eleven, drinking off some of the day's stress, y'know. He'll back me up. He'll always back me up."

The second suspect was named Edwin Burchfield. A former employee of Murray Blevins, he was a sour man in his late twenties, of average height and weight and wearing dark slacks and a button-down shirt. He had no prior arrests or convictions.

"I was a kitchen assistant at the Hind, yes. I live close by, on Sullivan Street. That was the only good thing about that darned place. The hours were endless, the pay was terrible, the chef was a real primadonna, and old Murray was a boring fool who'd bend your ear off about nothing given even a quarter of a chance. Yeah, you're right I didn't like it there much. I lasted about six months, until I managed to find something else to do. That was a year ago, maybe. Takes me longer to get to work now, but it's worth it. The Hind sucked. Last night? I finished work at about nine-thirty, and walked home. I was in by ten-fifteen. That's all."

The final suspect was a delivery man named Angus Hofstadter. He was of medium height but strongly built. He'd served a stretch of time in prison for breaking someone's legs. It was widely presumed that he'd been working for a debt enforcer at the time, but that wasn't ever proved. He was in his thirties, and had an oddly expressionless face.

"I have been into that restaurant once, but it's not really my sort of thing. I was checking out my delivery for this afternoon, Inspector. I've got a bunch of tables to take to a coffee shop a few doors down from that restaurant you mentioned. Actually, yeah,

I do often go and check places I'm going to deliver to, if they're unfamiliar. It can make your day go much smoother, and my boss, he doesn't like me wasting time. Be prepared, that's my motto. Besides, I like walking in the city at night. So after supper, I went to check out Eura & Paul, to make sure there was plenty of access, big enough doors, no road blockages, that sort of thing. It all looked fine."

When Hofstadter was escorted from the interview room, he was replaced by Officer Elden. "We've found the mask," he told the inspector. "It was in a trash bin a block from the Golden Hind. Abraham Lincoln, just like they said. There was a prop gun in there with it. Fake, but realistic. That was all, though. Apart from those two, the bin was empty."

"In that case," Inspector Parnacki said, "I'll need you to bring one of our suspects back in here, and I'll see if I can get a confession."

Who does Inspector Parnacki suspect and why?

HINTS

A) MURRAY BLEVINS HAD COMPREHENSIVE INSURANCE AGAINST LOSSES TO THEFT, PROVIDED THAT THE CASE ENDED IN A CONVICTION.

B) BUDDY CROSS WAS NOT ENTIRELY CORRECT ABOUT THE INFORMATION HE TOLD INSPECTOR PARNACKI.

C) MERLE WHEELER WAS IN THE RESTAURANT ALL EVENING, BUT THERE WERE PERIODS OF TIME WHEN HE WAS BUSY ASSISTING CUSTOMERS.

D) BALDWIN SWEET RATHER DISLIKES MERLE WHEELER.

E) RUBIN WILSON HAD USED HARLEY ROZELLA AS AN ALIBI ON NO FEWER THAN FOUR PREVIOUS OCCASIONS.

F) EDWIN BURCHFIELD WAS A POOR WORKER, AND HE DIDN'T LEAVE VOLUNTARILY—HE WAS FIRED BY MURRAY BLEVINS.

G) ANGUS HOFSTADTER STILL WORKS FOR CRIMINALS ON THE SIDE.

H) BARNEY DAVENPORT HOPES TO MOVE UP TO JUNIOR CHEF ONE DAY SOON.

Uncle Edmond

The evening sun glowed through the windows of the old gallery, lending it a lovely golden aura. Molly Holdway was in the oriental room at the far end, pacing back and forth in front of the cabinets. When the butler, McLemore, showed Miss Miller into the room, Molly gasped, and flew into her arms. "Mary, thank you so much for coming. I'm going out of my mind."

Miss Miller gave the younger woman a hug. "Why don't you tell me exactly what happened?"

"You know that my brother is named Porter? Oh, well, he is. He and Uncle Edmond have never been on good terms. Two weeks ago, Porter said something typically flippant, and Uncle took it very badly. Three days later, he sent a note saying that he'd finally decided with great reluctance to cut Porter out of his will, and how disappointed our mother would have been, and blah blah blah. Porter

just laughed it off, of course. He and Mother were very close, and he owns a printing firm which keeps him quite comfortably without any recourse to the family money. But Uncle called the rest of us—my cousins and me—here this weekend."

"You all came, of course."

"Of course. Even if he's horrid, he's still my uncle. But I admit I did rather envy Porter's lack of an invitation. Uncle was his usual critical self, but after he went to bed, the rest of us had a pleasant time. Breakfast was at seven-thirty, which isn't much fun at this time of year, but Uncle is very strict about meal times. Then at eight, he was found dead on the stairs with a knife in his neck. That would be bad enough, but the police arrested Porter at midday for Uncle's murder!"

"That's terrible," Miss Miller said.

"Yes! It's insane! Porter doesn't even kill *spiders*, and anyway, he wasn't here. But they've decided that he took revenge for being cut out of the will, and their only remaining interest appears to be gathering evidence to support their version of events. Unfortunately, Porter likes to take a long walk on Saturday and Sunday mornings—his 'constitutional'—and he was out of the house for an hour, so he doesn't even have Adele and the kids as his alibi. Uncle was very well connected of course, and I'm sure the police are under a lot of pressure to get the case solved immediately. I'm terrified something truly horrible is going to happen."

"I quite understand, my dear. Miscarriages of justice do happen. So who precisely was here this weekend, apart from yourself?"

"Myles cried off. Uncle never made any bones about not being related to him, so he leaves me to face the old beast on my own. I don't really blame him. Usually, I'd bring the children along, but I left them with him this time. I didn't want Uncle filling their heads with all sorts of nonsense about Porter. Anton is Uncle's eldest. He's here with Sybil and their children. Myles is the middle child. His wife, Edna, isn't here—she's with her mother. It's a shame. Edna is good value. Finally, Aline is the youngest of the three—I believe she's twenty-two this year. Boyd, her beau, never comes near this place. Father was Uncle's only sibling, so that's the lot of us. I suppose there's also the staff: McLemore the butler, a cook named Mrs. Codgill, three girls whose names I'm afraid I don't know, and a gardener, Mathis, and his boy. I don't suppose any one of us will be particularly saddened by our loss. Uncle was entirely too generous with his scorn. But it's difficult to imagine any of us committing murder."

"Were you in the house when the attack happened?"

A smile flickered over Molly's face. "You know me too well. No. I was out in the bowery, making the most of the chance to hear the local dawn chorus. I spotted a lovely late catbird, actually. The first I knew of the murder was when I got in at eight-thirty, looking for a nice cup of tea to warm me up."

"And what about your uncle's children?"

"No idea, I'm afraid. When we've talked, it's been about arrangements and practicalities. Mainly, we've sat around in dazed silence."

Miss Miller smiled. "Shall we go have a chat with them?"

Anton Pemmons was a reserved middle-aged man with thinning brown hair and a small toothbrush moustache. "Delighted to meet you, Miss Miller," he said. "I'm glad you're here to help Molly with this horrible situation."

"Thank you, Mr. Pemmons," Miss Miller said. "My condolences for your loss."

He sighed. "My father was a difficult man. Petty, vindictive, often wilfully cruel. Perhaps he was not always so, but I do not remember him otherwise. I will mourn him, but, heaven help me, I will not miss him."

"How was his relationship with Porter Boling?"

"My cousin is a cheerful, kindly, free-spirited man who cannot bear ill-talk of those he is fond of, so he and my father disliked each other quite intensely. Father seemed to think his will was a source of power, but Porter never gave a fig for the old man's money. I'm amazed he wasn't cut out of the will before now. I certainly can't imagine him killing anyone, let alone an unhappy old man."

"Did you hear or see anything odd this morning?"

"Unfortunately not, no. After breakfast, Sybil and I brought the children back up to our rooms, and I read them a story. It's their reward for getting through an early breakfast without causing a fuss. We heard one of the maids screaming—it was Lorena, I believe—and I came to investigate, leaving Sybil to calm the children. Father was already dead, with a blade planted in his throat. He looked extremely annoyed, even in death. McLemore had already gone for help. It wasn't long before the police arrived."

Myles Pemmons was in early middle age. Where Anton was rigorously neat, his brother had an air of dissipation about him. His clothes were a little too showy, his hair a little too long, his expression a little too sarcastic. On top of that, he didn't seem entirely sober.

"Mary Miller? You're Marilyn Hunt's birdwatching friend! She speaks very highly of your wisdom. Her nephew Ellis is significantly less warm."

Miss Miller put on a smile. "Guilty as charged, I'm afraid."

"I never did understand birdwatching," Myles said. "No idea

what Molly sees in it. All that . . . nature."

"It keeps us out of mischief," Miss Miller said pleasantly, ignoring Molly's frown. "You've heard about Mr. Boling's arrest, I assume?"

"Yes. Poor Porter. I wouldn't have thought him the type. Just goes to show. Frankly, he did us all a great favour. The rest of us should pool an inheritance together for him from our own shares. If they don't execute him, of course."

Miss Miller placed a calming hand on Molly's forearm, and gave her a little squeeze. The woman sighed, and forced herself to relax. "Did you see or hear anything unusual?"

"Not a thing. I was in the old gallery, watching the sun rise. Weekends here are always a significant trial, Mary. A moment of peace is to be treasured." He sagged, his smirk dissolving. "To be quite frank with you, my father never liked me very much. Anton tried hard, and Aline was young and sweet, while I was just annoying. I got away from the old buzzard the very instant I was able, and have returned here only reluctantly over the years. Just the sight of him sets my teeth on edge. I often seem to suffer him in my dreams, so I've always done my level best not to have any. Sometimes, I get scared that I'll end up the same way—bitter, spiteful, evil-minded, an old fool who has to bribe his flesh and blood to tolerate his company for a few hours."

"I'd say that being aware of the risk is half the battle," Miss Miller said kindly. "Thank you for your time."

Aline Pemmons was an attractive young woman. She managed to summon a pleasant smile for Miss Miller despite her troubled demeanour. "It's nice to meet you," she said. "Molly is lucky to have you as a friend." She turned to Molly. "I'm so sorry about Porter, Moll. I don't understand. I don't seem to understand anything today."

"I'm sorry for your loss," Miss Miller said.

"Thank you. I want to be sad. I really do. He was my father, and he taught me it was possible to love someone without liking them even a little. I'm not sad, though. The idea of facing the world knowing he's not there in the background causing problems, well, it's peculiar. Intimidating. This is a very confusing day. I can't really work out what the sun thought it was doing shining as usual. His death is a loss. It's just one I can't yet fathom."

Miss Miller gave her an encouraging smile. "Be gentle with yourself, my dear. Let it sink in at its own pace. The future will take care of itself."

"Thank you. I shall."

"Did you hear or see anything unusual this morning?"

Aline shook her head. "No, nothing. I'm afraid I was in the small drawing room, absorbed in Mr. Wells's latest scientific romance. It's a rather odd affair, even by his elevated standards. But it's absorbing enough, comet or no. The first hint I had of a problem was when the screaming started. That was Judith, I believe. Ever since then, I've half-expected to wake up."

"You've been very helpful, my dear. Thank you for your time," Miss Miller said.

As they headed back downstairs, Molly turned to Miss Miller.

"Should we talk to Judith next, then? I think she's the blonde girl. I truly doubt she'd stab anyone, but I suppose you never know."

"Oh, my dear, I already know who killed your uncle. It's just a matter of gathering a little more material to support some more pointed questions."

Who does Miss Miller suspect and why?

HINTS

A) THE PEMMONS FAMILY MONEY CAME FROM THE MANUFACTURE AND SALE OF GUNS AND AMMUNITION.

B) SYBIL PEMMONS, ANTON'S WIFE, DESPISED HER FATHER-IN-LAW WITH EVERY FIBRE OF HER BEING.

C) MYLES PEMMONS IS NOT ON PARTICULARLY GOOD TERMS WITH HIS WIFE, EDNA.

D) ANTON PEMMONS ALWAYS FELT EXTREMELY GUILTY THAT HE WASN'T GOOD ENOUGH FOR HIS FATHER, EVEN THOUGH HE INTELLECTUALLY KNEW THAT IT WAS IMPOSSIBLE TO BE SO.

E) APART FROM MYLES AND HIS FATHER, EDNA PEMMONS IS VERY FOND OF THE REST OF THE FAMILY.

F) JUDITH OFTEN FANTASIZED ABOUT MURDERING EDMOND PEMMONS, BUT WAS FAR TOO LAW-ABIDING EVER TO GO AHEAD WITH IT.

G) ALINE PEMMONS TENDS TO FORGET THAT REALITY EXISTS WHEN SHE'S READING. SHE HAS AT LEAST ONE COPY OF EVERYTHING H. G. WELLS HAS EVER RELEASED.

H) MOLLY HOLDWAY IS INCORRECT ABOUT HER BROTHER'S FEELINGS REGARDING BEING CUT OUT OF EDMOND'S WILL.

I) PORTER BOLING ONCE COMPETED IN A MARATHON AND DID RATHER WELL, A FACT WHICH HE KEPT COMPLETELY SECRET FROM HIS FAMILY AND FRIENDS.

J) MISS MILLER SAW ENOUGH TO BE CERTAIN THAT THE KILLER WAS LYING TO HER.

The High-flyer

It wasn't hard to guess that the dead man had been writing the word "HELP" in the sand with his finger when he'd run out of time, and his final letter trailed off pitifully. The sea had washed away a portion of the initial "H" as well, and with the lifeless hand and arm just lying there, it made for a very powerful photograph. It was a testament to the frailty of human endeavor,

and to the tragedy of murder. Josh's editor at the *Sentinel*, Reuben Marley, was overjoyed with the shot, and even went so far as to give Adam Matthews, the photographer, a nice little bonus. Josh's task was to get a suitably poignant story to go with the image.

The dead man was Clem Suttles, a wealthy middle-aged industrialist of minor repute. He'd been found dead on a beach outside the city. According to Pete down at the police station, he'd suffered multiple stab wounds. There was no sign of the murder weapon. In addition to his personal effects, Suttles had been carrying a note with a time and the name of the beach, sealed with a lipstick kiss.

In the absence of a spouse or child, Josh first went to speak to Suttles's business partner, Linwood Preston. The two men shared a suite of offices from which they managed their assorted collection of businesses. Their holding company was called Sutton Holdings, and was located in an expensive serviced office building downtown.

After a short wait in a handsomely furnished and decorated reception room, Josh was shown into Preston's office. The man was tall and thin, with very short grey hair and cold eyes.

Josh pulled his shoulders back and put on the barely perceptible smile he reserved for uptight business folks. "Joshua Cole, from the *Sentinel*. Thank you for agreeing to talk to me, sir."

"How may I help the fourth estate, Mr. Cole? It is a busy morning, as I'm sure you can imagine."

"Yes, sir. I just wanted to ask you a few questions about Clem Suttles."

"It's a tragedy, of course. Mr. Suttles was popular with his colleagues, and well-loved by those who knew him as a friend. He leaves a void in all our hearts. In the sixteen years that I knew him, he was never less than a canny businessman and a tireless champion for Sutton Holdings. His loss is a challenging blow, but we shall do honor to his legacy by moving on in the manner in which he would have wanted. Ultimately, we will continue to prosper, and keep growing stronger."

"Can you think of anyone who might have wished to harm him?"

"No one here, certainly. Sutton Holdings is a family, and his death is sad for all of us."

"What about outside the company?"

"No, of course not. Sutton Holdings is scrupulously fair and honest in all dealings. By being an ethical and morally upstanding business, we ensure smooth relationships with all our clients and partners. No one who had met Mr. Suttles would ever have wished him harm."

"I see. Thank you. Can you tell me what he was like as a man?"

"Of course. He had a keen eye for detail and a great capacity for solving problems and coming up with new ideas. Meetings were a particular strength, as he was confident and skilled at the simple presentation of complex material. He was tidy, punctual, and always well dressed. Very professional."

"Was he working on anything new or controversial at the moment?"

"Mr. Cole, I've been very patient, but I'm sure you understand that I'm not going to discuss company business with you. I'm afraid I'm going to have to get back to work. My assistant can show you out." He thumped a bell on his desk, and a short, dark-haired younger man appeared at the office door. "Mr. Dellinger, Mr. Cole was just leaving."

"Thank you for your time, Mr. Preston," Josh said. He stood, and followed the assistant out of the office. "Mr. Dellinger, was it?" he asked, once the door was closed.

"Yes, sir. Ramon."

"I'm Josh, Ramon. I get the feeling your boss wasn't very fond of Clem Suttles."

"Oh, no, that's not the case. Mr. Preston got on perfectly well with Mr. Suttles. I was assistant to both of them. But Mr. Preston doesn't believe in mixing work with sociability, while Mr. Suttles was always much chummier and more accessible."

"Am I correct that Mr. Suttles didn't have much time for women?"

Ramon looked alarmed. "No, sir, not at all."

Josh hid his grin. "He didn't have a wife," he said, suggestively.

"No, but he had someone special."

"A woman?"

"Of course."

"I see," Josh said. "Thank you for clearing that up."

"I wouldn't want you getting the wrong idea about Mr. Suttles." Ramon's voice had noticeably chilled.

"I understand. Your loyalty is a credit. I can see myself out from here, thank you."

Suttles's sister, Hattie Martin, lived in a pleasant area. Her house was freshly painted, with a neat garden that clearly emphasized order over creativity. Mrs. Martin was in early middle age, with the wary, worn-down look Josh associated with the parents of teenage children. She reluctantly agreed to talk to him, and sat him down in the kitchen while she prepared some coffee.

"What was Clem like?" Josh asked.

"He was my brother, and I'll miss him, but he was a bit of an idiot. Sure, he was smart, but he was always cocky. Convinced that he could do no wrong, and that everything would come up roses for him every time." She set down the coffee, and joined him at the table. "He could be very charming when he wanted to be, but he was ferociously petty if he didn't get his own way. All his friends were always like that, too—full of self-congratulation and self-indulgence. By the age of fourteen, he was bragging about how rich he was going to be. He was well on his way, too. But risks always backfire in the end."

"Risks?" Josh took a swig of his coffee.

"Clem loved taking chances, Mr. Cole. He was an unrepentant gambler, both professionally and recreationally. He particularly liked it when his victories led to painful losses for someone else. That's the trouble with being smart and vain, but emotionally dumb—you always believe you'll be good enough to get out of trouble. Being manipulative served him well in business, but I always suspected it would catch up to him in the end."

"Do you know if he was involved in any shady business dealings?"

"I'm sure of it. He always was, one way or another. But I don't know anything specific, I'm afraid."

"And did you ever meet his business partner?"

"The Preston fellow? No. I knew he existed, but from what I gathered, he's a very cold fish. Didn't socialize."

"I see. Was Clem involved with anyone romantically?"

Hattie nodded. "A woman named Katherine. I met her a couple of times. She was very pretty. He'd been seeing her for about a year, which was really serious by Clem's usual standards."

"I don't suppose you know how I can contact her?"

"No idea, no."

"You've been very helpful. Thanks for your time."

Josh left Hattie's house, frustrated. It seemed that his last hope of finding something moving to hang a story off was going to be Suttles's girlfriend. There wasn't anything particularly touching in the death of a manipulative narcissist.

It took a little bit of digging, but eventually Josh tracked down

Katherine, surname Norwood, to a quiet street not far from a large park. Her house was modest, but looked well cared for. A beautiful, sad-faced woman in her twenties answered the door when he knocked.

"Katherine Norwood? My name is Joshua Cole, from the *Sentinel*."

The woman's face twisted in panic. Josh immediately jammed his foot in the open doorway, wincing as the door bounced off his shoe.

"I just want to ask you a few questions about Clem Suttles, Katherine," he said.

"Go *away*," she hissed, trying to close the door again.

"This is your chance to tell me your side," Josh said, trying to make his voice soothing. "If you want us to go to print without your version of things . . ."

She sagged brokenly. "Very well."

Inside the house, the reason for her fear was obvious. It was clear that she was Mrs. Norwood, not Miss Norwood. She clutched at Josh's arm as they went into the lounge. "You *have* to leave my name out of the paper, Mr. Cole. You have to. My husband has no idea. This could destroy both our lives."

"Well, if I had something more interesting to print, that might be possible," Josh said.

"Oh, Lord. I don't know what I can tell you that would do. Wilhelm is a good provider, but he's just not stimulating company. Clem was attractive, well off, exciting. I couldn't help myself."

"Where did you meet?"

"At a company drinks evening. Clem owns the firm that Willi works for. He noticed me there. Soon after that, Willi got a promotion that involved a lot of regular business trips. I knew what Clem was doing, and I suppose I welcomed it. Most weeks, Willi is away for at least a few days. He's away this week. Clem took me to places I'd never dreamed of. I knew he'd get bored sooner or later, but it was so much fun while it lasted. I never dreamed it would end like this. Please, please, don't mention my name. Willi would go absolutely insane."

"What can you tell me about Clem as a person?"

"He's charming, clever, a bit of a gambler, quite ruthless about getting what he wants. He was going big places, I think. I can't honestly say he was very nice, but he definitely knew his way around a good time. I wasn't in love with him, and I'm sure he cheated on me from time to time, but I'm really going to miss him."

Josh frowned. "What about his past?"

"He didn't talk about his childhood much. I met his sister a couple of times. She seemed pleasant enough. But really, Clem was focused on his work, because it was his channel to advance himself."

"Do you think he was going to make it?"

"Oh, yes. Undoubtedly. He was resourceful and determined. Another ten years, and he'd have been one of the leaders of the city's business community."

"I see. Well, I have to get on. Thanks for talking to me,

Katherine."

"You'll leave my name out of your story?"

He nodded. "Sure." *Probably*, he added to himself. She'd be more interesting as a "mysterious beauty", anyway.

Later, back at his desk, Josh was pulling together a story painting Clem as a rising star of the business world cut down in his prime when he dropped his pen and swore loudly. As colleagues turned to look, he picked up his telephone and called Pete down at the station. "I know who murdered Clem Suttles," he said.

Who does Josh suspect, and why?

HINTS

A) CLEM SUTTLES ACTIVELY ENJOYED CAUSING EMOTIONAL PAIN TO OTHER PEOPLE.

B) LINWOOD PRESTON'S PERSONAL LIFE WAS BROADLY THE SAME AS HIS WORK LIFE—REGIMENTED AND FAIRLY STERILE.

C) RAMON DELLINGER WAS NOT PARTICULARLY FOND OF EITHER OF HIS BOSSES.

D) KATHERINE NORWOOD WAS GENUINELY TERRIFIED OF THE CONSEQUENCES OF BEING OUTED AS CLEM'S LOVER.

E) HATTIE MARTIN HAD A COMPLEX RELATIONSHIP WITH HER BROTHER AND SECRETLY, ON BALANCE, SUSPECTED THAT THE WORLD WAS BETTER OFF WITHOUT HIM IN IT.

F) WHEN HE DIED, CLEM HAD BEEN PLANNING TO WRITE AN "M" NEXT.

G) SUTTON HOLDINGS HAD BANKRUPTED NO FEWER THAN SEVEN BUSINESS OWNERS AND RIVALS.

The Note

The death of thirty-five-year-old Clark Payne had a number of puzzling elements to it, and these did not get much clearer as further details emerged. His body had been found on Friday morning in his brother Evan's house, by a cleaner who came twice a week. He had been dead for at least a day, but did not appear to be wounded. Among his effects was a suicide note, unsigned, which did not seem to be in his own handwriting. On the table beside the couch the body was found on were a packet of sleeping pills and a bottle of scotch.

While specialists examined the body and the scene of the crime for evidence, Inspector Parnacki decided to start by visiting Clark's own home and speaking to his widow, Inga.

Like that of his brother, Clark Payne's house was comfortable, and conveyed modest prosperity. Slightly shabby trimmings suggested that either money had been a little tight recently, or that Clark had been comparatively frugal. Inga met the inspector at the door, dressed in an expensive mourning gown. She was in her early thirties, but little pinch-lines around her mouth made her look older. She waited for Parnacki to speak, watching him with undisguised disapproval.

"Mrs. Payne? My name is Inspector Parnacki, and I'm investigating your husband's death. May I speak with you?"

"I know your name." Her voice was slightly hoarse.

He forced a smile. "A newspaper, probably."

"A celebrity, are you then?"

"Just a policeman, madam."

She turned away. "Come in, if that's what you want."

The inspector followed her into a sitting room, and took a place on a fading sofa.

Mrs. Payne frowned at him. "So?"

"When did you last see your husband, Mrs. Payne?"

She shrugged. "Wednesday morning." There was a pause. "I thought he was on a business trip. He was supposed to be out of the city until Saturday morning."

"And what business would that be?"

"Ironmongery supplies. Tools. Bolts. Nails. All that nonsense. Deathly dull."

"I see. So you don't know why he was at his brother's house?"

"I can't imagine any legitimate reason."

The inspector looked up at that. "You suspect an illegitimate one?"

"Isn't it obvious? Evan murdered my

husband, Mr. Inspector Paddington Parnacki."

Suppressing a wince, he said, "Why would he do such a thing?"

"Why else? Money. My mother-in-law is not much longer for this world. God knows how she's clung on so long past the point of reason. When she finally shuffles off to her just rewards, my father-in-law's estate will finally be released. Evan clearly wants it all for himself. His rubber sheeting firm is having a hard time. He lured Clark to his home under false pretences, and murdered him there."

"It's my understanding that Evan Payne is out of the city at the moment."

She sneered. "Makes a great alibi, doesn't it?"

"Do you have any proof of any of this?"

"Of course not. But it's so simple a child could see it."

The inspector nodded. "It's certainly an avenue I'll be exploring. Can you think of anyone else who might have had a grudge against your husband?"

"His business partner Lewis would love to have the firm all to himself. He'll be delighted. Oh, he was all very friendly on the surface, but I never trusted him an inch. His eyes are too close together. Nasty, ratty little man."

The inspector thanked Mrs. Payne, and made his exit. With Evan Payne still not at home or at his office, Inspector Parnacki turned next to the dead man's business partner, Lewis Askew. There was in fact very little of the rat about the man, although in fairness to Mrs. Payne, his eyes were slightly closer together than was usual. He seemed greatly preoccupied, and anxious to talk to someone about it.

"Clark's death is the worst possible news," he told the inspector. "He was a good friend. I've known him since college. We went into business together because I was good at finances but not people, and Clark was the obverse."

"And how has business been?"

"Truthfully, we've been struggling. It's only Clark's charm and bullishness that's kept our main clients loyal to us. I think my best hope now is to try to sell the company quickly before we lose all our value entirely. I want to grieve for my friend, but I'm panicking too much about my livelihood and my mortgage payments."

"I'm sorry to hear that," the inspector said. "What can you tell me about Clark's relationships with the people around him?"

"Well, he wasn't close to his brother Evan. They were very different people, and merely tolerated their blood bond with each other. I wouldn't say that there was any dislike there, just a certain weary lack of interest. It always seemed a shame. Then there was his wife Inga, of course."

"Yes," Inspector Parnacki said.

"Ah. You've met her, I see. She can be a bit of a strain sometimes. She was sweet when she was young, but I suppose life didn't go as she'd planned. Another shame. She's been increasingly sour for the last ten years. Their relationship has been stormy for quite a long time now. Which reminds me . . . I suppose you have to know. For the last few months, Clark had been carrying on an affair with a mysterious younger woman named Em, short for Emma, I think. He never gave me any details. She'd brightened his life up considerably, although apparently she was also a source of some concern."

"Oh?"

"Yes. Usually when he was talking about her, he'd glow. But sometimes he'd get nervous, scared even. I've no idea why, however. He wouldn't talk about the details. I occasionally wondered if she was a mob boss's daughter or something exotic like that."

"I see. Can you think of any enemies Mr. Payne might have had? Anyone who would have wanted to have hurt him?"

"Hardly. There is a lamentably influential banker who loathes both Clark and Evan, and has done since they were children. Roland Cameron, his name is. Clark placed many of his woes at Roland's feet, and Lord knows the man throttled our lines of credit quite effectively. He does his best to make life difficult for them both. But actual harm, even murder? I can't credit it."

By the time that Inspector Parnacki returned to the station, preliminary reports were available regarding the crime scene and the body. Vance Washburn was the primary point of contact for the forensic evidence, and he joined Parnacki in his office to discuss what was known.

"The cause of death was asphyxiation," Detective Washburn said. "There was no indication of any sort of struggle, even at the most superficial level. At first we thought maybe he had been overcome by natural gas, but the actual cause of death proved to be nitrogen oversaturation."

"Nitrogen? Really?" the inspector asked.

"It's not difficult to obtain, just costly. Because nitrogen is the largest component of air, the body doesn't register pure nitrogen as a threat. There's none of the lung-burning sensations you'd normally associate with asphyxiation. It's a quick and painless way to die. There was an empty industrial canister hidden behind a book-case. The canister's valve was fitted with a rather clever clockwork timer device. It does appear as if supplies were laid in to make the room somewhat airtight—draught excluders, nails, tape, and so on—and these do appear recent, but they were not used."

"Obvious tampering and a gas cylinder hardly gel with a suicide note."

Washburn nodded. "Quite."

The following morning, Evan Payne finally turned up. Inspector Parnacki showed him into the office.

"Thank you for coming, Mr. Payne."

"I'm sorry I couldn't get here sooner. I've been visiting my mother this week. As soon as I heard the news, I came back to the city. Do I understand that

Clark was found in my house?"

"I'm afraid so," the inspector said. "Do you have any idea what Clark could have been doing there?"

Evan shook his head blankly. "Absolutely none. We have each other's keys stored away, in case of emergency, so I suppose that's how he got in. But the why is totally beyond me."

"How was your relationship with your brother?"

"Cordial enough. We weren't particularly close, but he was family. I certainly had nothing against him."

"You said you were with your mother?"

"Yes. She's been a bit dotty for a couple of years now, and she's getting very frail. There's a full-time nurse who looks after her, Mrs. Stevens. I thought I should spend some time up there while I still could. I don't know if Mother knew it was me, but at least I was there. I'm getting married in a couple of months, and this might be the last chance I have to get up there this year. I don't know how long she has."

"Forgive my asking, but do you know the provisions of your mother's will?"

Evan laughed bitterly. "Ah, you've been talking to Inga. My father was quite well off, and left what he had in trust to Mother, the remainder to come to Clark and me after she died. Mother's care has been expensive, and neither of us ever begrudged her a penny. There's a small sum of money left. Nothing worth killing over, if money ever is. Mother might not be able to verify I was with her, but Mrs. Stevens will."

"I see. And can you tell me anything about Roland Cameron?"

"Rotten Roland?" Evan blinked. "He's a banker. I accidentally broke his arm rather badly when I was eight and he and Clark were six. I felt dreadful about it. Unfortunately, it never set quite right, and he still hasn't forgiven us. He's a banker now, and uses the little clout he has to try to lash out at us in frankly rather pathetic ways. He's no killer, Inspector. Just a damned fool."

"That's all for now," Parnacki said. "Thank you for coming in." Once Payne was gone, the inspector went over to Detective Washburn's desk. "Any sign of intoxicants in the victim's stomach or blood?"

Washburn shook his head. "No, nothing."

"In that case, I think I know who killed him."

Who does Inspector Parnacki suspect, and why?

HINTS

A) EVAN PAYNE NEVER DRANK SCOTCH.

B) INGA PAYNE WAS NOT PARTICULARLY DISTRESSED BY THE DEATH OF HER HUSBAND.

C) THE CANISTER'S TIMER HAD NOT PERFORMED AS INTENDED.

D) MRS. STEVENS TOOK ADVANTAGE OF EVAN'S PRESENCE TO HAVE THE EVENING OFF WHILE HE WAS UP THERE.

E) LEWIS ASKEW WAS ONCE PROPOSITIONED—UNSUCCESSFULLY—BY INGA PAYNE.

F) EVAN'S MOTHER LUCILLE NO LONGER UNDERSTOOD WHO HE WAS DURING HIS VISITS.

G) EVAN'S FIANCÉE, MARIANNE MILTON, HAD BEEN SAD TO HEAR OF CLARK'S DEATH.

H) MATERIALS HAD BEEN ASSEMBLED TO MAKE EVAN'S LOUNGE AIRTIGHT, BUT IT HADN'T BEEN COMPLETED.

I) EVAN AND CLARK'S INHERITANCE WAS WORTH AROUND A COUPLE OF YEARS OF ONE OF THEIR SALARIES.

J) THE CANISTER OF COMPRESSED NITROGEN CAME FROM A MANUFACTURER OF AGRICULTURAL PRODUCTS.

K) BY THE TIME THE CLEANER ARRIVED, THE NITROGEN/OXYGEN BALANCE IN THE ROOM HAD NORMALIZED.

The Heirloom Ring

The Grand Hotel made every effort to live up to its name. The carpets were thick and richly hued, the fittings were a tasteful blend of chrome and gilt, and the foyer was adorned with enough statues, paintings and floral displays to satisfy even the fussiest client. The staff darted back and forth like fish in an exotic reef, their outfits a breezy blend of white and sky-blue. All told, it was an unusually pleasant setting for a conference about a board game.

Miss Miller took a sip of her tea, which was acceptable if undistinguished, and looked around the foyer. If there were chess people milling around during their lunchtime, they were difficult to pick out from the rest of the guests, who were all as smart and well-attended as the location would normally demand. She heard footsteps, and looked around to see Shelton

Dole approaching. He gave her a quick smile, and sat down opposite her.

"Thank you for meeting me here, Mary," he said.

"My pleasure," she replied. "It's always nice to have an excuse to come down to the Grand. The room may be short on birds, but there's plenty of plumage to admire."

He smiled. A busboy hurried up to the table, and Shelton ordered a coffee from him.

"I understand you're not actually playing any chess at this conference of yours," Miss Miller said.

"Not officially, no. There are a number of talks and panels about certain elements of strategy like the double-rook sacrifice or the rolling pawn mass, historically interesting games such as the 1889 Lauer-Basker match, and so on. But there were a lot of games going on last night, I understand. I was somewhat distracted by that point."

"Of course. You mentioned a robbery. What exactly happened?"

"I was going to propose to Goldie last night, using my presence here at the conference as an excuse to get her to come here for dinner without suspicions. I inherited a lovely diamond ring from my grandmother, who knew I intended to put it to good use. It was valuable when she first acquired it, and time has only added to its worth. I had that in my valise, which was with all the other bags and coats at the back of the room. When the last panel finished at five, I saw that my bag had been opened. The ring case was missing, and obviously the ring with it."

"So someone removed it during the day?"

Shelton nodded. "It must have been after luncheon. I shared a lunch table with four fellows whom I know to varying degrees of familiarity. I took the ring out beforehand, so I could show it to them. Foolish, I know, but I was too excited at the prospect of proposing. I put it back when we went back into the main conference room. So it was definitely there at one forty-five."

"Could an outsider have come into the room?"

"Possible, but tricky. There's a fellow on the door who has been making sure that entry is granted to people who've subscribed to the weekend."

"So then it must be one of your chess people."

"I suppose so. But there are fifty of us here, and people are back and forth all the time, taking trips to relieve themselves, or procure drinks, or what-have-you. It wouldn't have looked odd to have someone head over to the bags. Anyone could have done it."

"Perhaps," Miss Miller said. "Is your valise still the one with that peewit stencilled on the front?"

"Yes, although given how much stick I've had at the ornithological society about it I've often considered obtaining a new case. It's a fascinating bird—noble-looking, far-ranging, and both fearless and fiendishly clever in dealing with enemies."

"Those things are all true. But you must admit that it also flies like a drunkard."

Shelton shrugged. "You can't have everything. Besides, the chess club people would never pay attention to anything as mundane as a bird on a case."

"There is that," Miss Miller said. "So with respect to your

missing ring, the obvious conclusion is that one of your luncheon partners is likely to have robbed you. How would anyone else know that you had the ring on you?"

He sighed. "I suppose so, yes. I didn't really want to admit it to myself, but your logic is inescapable."

"Have you spoken about the theft to any of them?"

"I have not, I'm afraid. I hope you'll forgive me."

"My dear Shelton, there's nothing to forgive. You did the right thing. I assume you can contrive a reason to snatch a few minutes with each of your lunch partners and bring them out for me to have a quick word with? I'll think of something plausibly innocent."

"That will be easy enough. They're not in one group at the moment, so I'll just ask them individually for their assistance in a delicate matter. You know at least one of them already, actually—Olly Griffith."

"How pleasant," Miss Miller said. "Please, ferry your suspects forth and we shall see what we can do."

A few minutes later, Shelton was back with his companion, an unfamiliar little man with thick spectacles whom he introduced as Osgood Tinsley.

"A pleasure to meet you, Mr. Tinsley," she said.

"Likewise, Miss Miller. How may I be of service?"

"Well, it's a little embarrassing," she said. "You were here at the Grand yesterday afternoon, as I understand it?"

"Yes, I was indeed."

"Did you happen to spot a very tall man dressed in a bright

red jacket anywhere? He'd be impossible to mistake. He's almost six foot six in height and bald as an egg, but with the most magnificent curling silver moustaches that stick out a good inch past his ears."

"My word," Tinsley said. "Yes, he does sound extremely distinguished. I would certainly remember him. Unfortunately, I was in the conference room for most of the time. I did come out once, to make use of the facilities, but I certainly didn't see anyone of that description. May I ask why you're looking for him?"

"It's a . . . delicate matter," Miss Miller replied. "Thank you so much, Mr. Tinsley. I'm sorry to have wasted your time."

"Not at all," he replied, covering his bewilderment with a polite smile, and allowing Shelton to whisk him away.

A moment later, Shelton was back. "Did that help?"

"Oh yes," Miss Miller said, with a smile. "Now we have an idea of his movements, and he is little the wiser."

"Who was it you were describing? Some figment of your imagination?"

"My grandfather, Chelford Miller. Since he's been dead for around forty years, I feel relatively safe in assuming that none of your companions will have

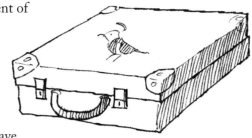

spotted him hanging around the hotel yesterday."

"Yes," Shelton said. "An excellent choice."

The next man that Shelton brought along was very familiar. Miss Miller stood up to greet him warmly. "Dear Olly. How are you? I didn't know you were interested in chess."

Oliver Griffith was tall and long-faced, with unusually mobile eyebrows. He was a keen birder. "Mary, what a lovely surprise. I wouldn't have thought to find you in the company of chess players. How the mighty have fallen!"

"Oh, I dabbled a little in my youth," she said. "I prefer real life, however. Just as unpredictable, and it requires less staring at inanimate objects. I prefer to stare at the animate."

Olly smiled. "Speaking of which, will you be at the ornithological society dinner next month?"

"Of course. I assume both of you gentlemen will be in attendance as well?"

"That we shall," Shelton said.

"Quite right," said Oliver. "Now, to what do we owe the pleasure of your visit here, my dear?"

Miss Miller repeated the description of her grandfather, and delicately implied that she was attempting to trace his movements.

"Hm. No, I definitely didn't see anyone like that. I was in the conference for the whole afternoon, however. Doesn't seem much point in subscribing to the weekend and then not paying attention. So honestly, he could have been doing war-dances in the lobby here for all I know."

"I appreciate it," Miss Miller said. "I'll let you get back to luncheon, and I'll see you next month."

The next fellow, Sandy Cooper, was unfamiliar. He looked a little like a fox, with bushy, slicked-back hair, and a quite creditable moustache. He listened to Miss Miller's description, and then shook his head thoughtfully. "I think I can be reasonably confident in saying that your fellow wasn't here, my dear."

"Oh?" she asked.

"I'm afraid I found yesterday afternoon dreadfully dull, and I ended up spending most of it at the bar. I did stick my head back in a few times, but it just wasn't for me. Shame, really. There wasn't an awful lot to do other than put a dent in their excellent port supply, and observe the comings and goings. Your chap was not among them."

"I see. Yes, that does sound fairly conclusive. That's a big help, Mr. Cooper. Thank you."

"Any time, my dear lady."

The final arrival was definitely familiar. Miss Miller watched him approach, and finally placed him shortly before Shelton made the introductions. Elwood Hembry had been a member of the ornithological society for a short period a couple of years earlier. Asthma had forced him to retire soon after. She remembered him as a polite, modest man.

"Yes, of course I remember you, Miss Miller. I never forget a face. How lovely to see you again. I hope the early mornings are still yielding their avian secrets readily."

"Thank you, yes," she said. "Now, please forgive me for disturbing your luncheon. I was wondering if you might be able to assist me with something." She repeated her description.

"I wasn't out of the conference for long yesterday afternoon," Hembry said. "However, I did pop out at one point. My wife brought over some notes I'd promised to a friend, but had left at home. I certainly didn't see any such fellow while I was out of the room. The last time I saw anyone even vaguely fitting that description was the March before last, in a park."

"I see," Miss Miller said. "Well, thank you very much for your time. It seems I must take my hunt elsewhere."

A few minutes later, Shelton returned. "Forgive me if I seem dubious," he said, "but I can't see that helped us at all."

"Just the contrary," Miss Miller said. "I'm reasonably sure I know who stole your ring."

Who does Miss Miller suspect, and why?

HINTS

A) SHELTON DOLE WAS FAR MORE CONCERNED ABOUT THE MISSING RING'S SENTIMENTAL VALUE THAN ABOUT ITS PRICE.

B) OSGOOD TINSLEY WAS A MASTERFUL STRATEGIST, AND PROBABLY THE BEST CHESS PLAYER AT THE CONFERENCE THAT WEEKEND.

C) OLIVER GRIFFITH WAS NOT A WEALTHY MAN.

D) SANDY COOPER WOULD NOT HAVE DESCRIBED SHELTON DOLE AS A FRIEND.

E) ELWOOD HEMBRY WAS NOT EXAGGERATING HIS FACILITY FOR FACES.

F) THE GRAND HOTEL'S SECURITY WAS SURPRISINGLY INEFFECTUAL, AND THE HOTEL SUFFERED FOUR THEFTS OVER THE WEEKEND OF THE CHESS CONFERENCE.

G) A LOT OF MONEY WAS RIDING ON SOME OF THE GAMES THAT CERTAIN CONFERENCE MEMBERS PLAYED.

H) MISS MILLER HAD GIVEN UP PLAYING CHESS BECAUSE NO ONE SHE KNEW WAS ABLE TO BEAT HER, AND IT BECAME BORING.

Anastasia

The victim—Anastasia Eldridge, 23—was found in her bathroom. According to the notes that Inspector Parnacki had received, she'd been in the process of dyeing her hair when she was attacked. There'd been a short struggle, if the state of the room was any indicator. Flecks of hair dye spattered the walls and floor, whipped around by her long hair. The cause of death was strangulation with a thin rope, not present at the scene. The victim's bathrobe was done up, and there was no evidence of sexual assault or any attempt to cause pain. Entrance to her apartment had been gained by way of a crowbar or similar device that had jimmied the front door open. Given where the victim was found, it seemed likely that she hadn't heard the modest amount of noise that it would have made.

Neighbours claimed not to have heard any disturbance. It was the broken door that had alerted Warren Horner, who lived across the hall in the apartment opposite. He'd sought police assistance at 7.30pm, and he'd been there with them when they'd found the body. There had been very little in the way of evidence relating to the crime recovered from the scene. By far the most useful resource had been the victim's extremely detailed and extensive social diary, from which the officers working the case had compiled a long list of suspects. Miss Eldridge had recently left her employment as a hostess in a salon, a job which she'd switched to after failing to gain any particular success as a chorus girl. According to her diary, she had been living off savings and gifts while attempting to find other options for employment.

The various suspects and persons of interest were scheduled for questioning over the course of a long morning. The inspector settled himself in an interview room with his pipe, a pouch of tobacco, and a large mug of the station's laughable attempt at coffee.

The first interview was with Warren Horner, the man who had reported the break-in. He was a dumpy-looking factory worker in his late forties, with receding grey hair and saggy jowls. He was wearing a cheap suit, and wringing his hands. The inspector welcomed him in and introduced himself.

"How would you describe your relationship with Miss Eldridge, Mr. Horner?"

"I lived next door to her, didn't I? We was friendly. Anastasia was a truly lovely young woman, with a bright smile for everyone. She brightened up the building. But I did worry about her."

"Why was that?"

"Well, beneath the smiles, she always looked a little bit sad, you know? Like there were things eating at her, and she was determined not to show it. She often went out in the evenings, all dolled up. I'd see her go. She had a number of, well, I won't say suitors, because I don't think they were. Admirers, maybe. I tried to look out for her, I really did. I was always worried something would happen to her. And now it has. She didn't deserve it."

"Were you at home at the time?"

"God help me, yes. I was reading about the French Revolution, as it happens. My Estelle died twenty years ago, so I do a lot of reading. I got to the end of a chapter, and peeked out the door to check everything was OK, and of course it wasn't. When she didn't answer my calling, I went to get someone as fast as I could, but it wasn't enough. If I hadn't been reading, maybe I'd have heard them break in. Maybe I could have helped to save her."

Craig Clabaugh was a reasonably good-looking milkman in his

mid-thirties. He was dressed in stylish casual clothing, and gave the inspector a roguish grin as he arrived.

"Yeah, I remember Anastasia," he said. "We had a little thing between us, maybe seven months ago. Well, not exactly little, if you know what I mean. But brief. She was a real sweetheart. I haven't seen her since, though."

"Where did you meet her?" the inspector asked.

"We met at a dance club, and hit it off straight away. Girls like Anastasia, there's vulnerability under the glitter. You've just got to listen to them, offer them some reassurance that they're incredible and amazing. That's all they really want. It's a small enough price, and the rewards are totally worth it."

"And where were you on the evening in question?"

"Walking the dog," Clabaugh said easily. "It's what I'm doing most evenings. I'm an early riser, so I'm early to bed most nights."

"Unless you're out dancing, I presume," said the inspector.

"Well yes, obviously not then."

"And did anyone you know see you while you were walking the dog?"

Clabaugh paused. "No."

"So you're saying you have no actual alibi for the time of Miss Eldridge's murder."

"Heck. Look, I was with someone. This mustn't get out, though. My wife, her husband . . . Yolanda Luttrell. She lives round the corner from me. Her husband likes to go out drinking, so I pop in there sometimes when the dog needs walking. She'll back me up."

The inspector took down Mrs. Luttrell's details, and assured Mr. Clabaugh that someone would be in contact.

The next person in was Alden Hance, Anastasia's regular boyfriend. He was in his mid-twenties, with a pronouncedly bookish air about him, even through his obvious grief. He was dressed in a tidy suit, with a restrained tie. According to the inspector's notes, he worked as an actuary for an insurance firm.

"I can't believe it's real," he told the inspector. "Ana and I grew up together. She was always a bright, dazzling thing. She'd had

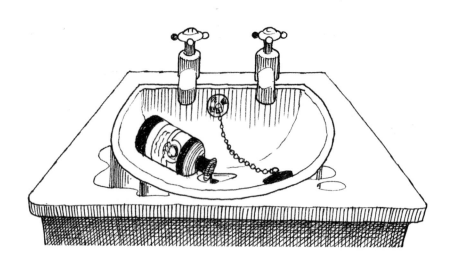

her fair share of problems and so on, but she worked so hard to overcome them all. She was always welcome at our home as a kid. My sister adored her. They'd have sleepovers sometimes, when Ana needed to get out of the house quickly. I was really proud for her when she got into showbusiness. We've been going steady for a couple of years now. I never could quite believe my luck. I asked her to marry me last year, but she said she'd promised herself that she'd go three years with someone before agreeing to be wed. I was going to ask her again on our third anniversary, make a nice gesture of it, a story to tell the kids."

"Did you see her often?"

"A couple of times a week. She worked very hard. She really wanted to make it in showbiz. It was fine. I knew her hours were crazy, and it didn't matter. I work long hours anyway."

The inspector nodded. "And where were you on the evening in question?"

Hance sighed. "Working, of course. I've been working until eight every night for the last ten days."

"Do you know if Miss Eldridge had any particular male friends?"

"Ana? No, not really. She was always popular, and the entertainment world is sociable, but her close friends were all girls. Why? Was there some chap at her work causing trouble?"

"Just a routine question," the inspector said. "Thanks for your time."

Gustavo Schultz was Anastasia's semi-secret lover. A business lawyer for a leading city firm, he was dressed in an expensive suit and white shirt, with a bright silk tie, white patent leather gloves, and highly polished Italian leather shoes. There was definitely a predatory air to him.

"Yes, poor Anastasia. I knew her very well, yes. She was in a rather precarious financial state, having left her job a couple of months ago. It gave me great pleasure to be able to help out someone so clearly deserving, as best I could. She was extremely grateful for the assistance."

"And would you have been so helpful if she'd been less . . . grateful?"

Schultz smiled. "Oh, I doubt it. I do abhor ingratitude."

"Are you married, Mr. Schultz?" asked the inspector.

"Engaged. My fiancée is named Zora Larue. She's a make-up artist."

"Does she know about Miss Eldridge's status as your lover?"

"She does."

"I see. How long has she been aware of the situation?"

"For as long as it's been going on. No, she's not delighted about it, but she knew who I was when she agreed to marry me."

The inspector nodded. The old saying usually came true: marry for money and you'll earn every penny. "Where were you on the night of the murder, Mr. Schultz?"

"I was having a drink with a client, in a bar downtown. I forget the name offhand, but I can check it and let you know. In case you were wondering, Zora was working. She's not attached to one specific venue, but she's in high demand, so she's almost always busy in the afternoons and early evenings. Again, I'm not precisely sure where she was working, but I'm sure I could find out."

The final interviewee was Cyril Tilson, the manager of the salon where Anastasia had worked until recently. He was a heavy man in his mid-fifties, with a spray of thin hair on his head and a nervous expression. He was wearing a reasonably expensive suit and shirt, but it didn't do much to improve his overall appearance. His handshake was somewhat clammy.

"I was very sad to hear about Annie," he said. "She was popular at the salon. Always had a nice smile. It was a shame that she decided to leave, but hostess work isn't for everyone. You gotta be patient and friendly, and prepared to do a lot of listening." He paused. "Look, I don't want you getting the wrong idea, Inspector. There's no funny business. Nothing illegal or immoral. Just people looking for a nice girl who'll bring drinks and then hang around to talk to them about their day. You understand?"

"I'm sure your establishment is perfectly reputable, Mr. Tilson," the inspector said.

"Yeah. Reputable. That's us. So, yeah, Anastasia was a loss. She didn't say why she was leaving, but I got the feeling she found a better gig. More money, fewer hours. I didn't pry. First thing you learn in my line, no prying. Like I said, being a hostess ain't for everyone."

"Where were you on the evening of the murder?"

"Look, I know you gotta ask, but it wasn't me, OK? I'm a fat old man, and my life is full of beautiful girls with problems. I try not to be one of them. Why would I risk hurting one? Anyway,

I was out recruiting. Most of my girls, they come off the chorus lines, fed up of mistreatment and earning pennies. So I was at the Royal, I reckon. Plenty of people could put me in the bar there."

When Tilson had left, Inspector Parnacki lit his pipe, looked down at his notes, and circled a name. "Let's see you try to wriggle out of this," he said.

Who does Inspector Parnacki suspect, and why?

HINTS

A) HAVING HAD A VERY DIFFICULT CHILDHOOD, ANASTASIA ELDRIDGE HAD NOT GROWN UP TO BECOME A WELL-ADJUSTED YOUNG WOMAN.

B) WARREN HORNER, ANASTASIA'S NEIGHBOUR, USED TO WATCH HER BOTH THROUGH HIS WINDOW, WHICH LOOKED OUT ONTO THE STREET, AND THROUGH THE SECURITY HOLE IN HIS DOOR.

C) IN REALITY, CRAIG CLABAUGH VERY RARELY PERMITTED HIS DOG ANY SIGNIFICANT EXERCISE.

D) WHEN ANASTASIA ASKED ALDEN HANCE NOT TO COME TO HER PERFORMANCES IN CASE HER BOSS OBJECTED, HE WAS HAPPY TO AGREE. HE WASN'T A GREAT FAN OF LIVE

ENTERTAINMENT.

E) GUSTAVO SCHULTZ WAS GIVING ANASTASIA A WEEKLY SUM EQUAL TO THAT EARNED BY JUNIOR CLERKS IN HIS OFFICE.

F) ZORA LARUE WAS WELL AWARE OF HER FIANCÉ'S INFIDELITIES, AND BITTERLY HATED HIS INSISTENCE ON KEEPING HER INFORMED OF ALL HIS FOOLING AROUND.

G) CYRIL TILSON WAS A PLEASANT EMPLOYER TO WORK FOR, AND LIKE MOST OF THE HOSTESSES AT THE SALON, ANASTASIA WAS GENUINELY FOND OF HIM.

H) THE CROWBAR USED TO BREAK INTO ANASTASIA'S HOME WAS NEVER FOUND. NEITHER WAS THE CORD WITH WHICH SHE WAS STRANGLED.

Solutions

1. The Intruder .... page 10

The French windows in the lounge have been painted shut. Scott claimed to have found them open when he arrived. If they had been opened recently, the paint sealing them would have been cracked away. As it is intact, he must have been lying, and trying to imply that the killer was someone who did not have easy access to the victim. Faced with the error in his account, he confessed, and became openly gleeful at having finally found the nerve to take revenge for his mother's death.

2. The Bowers Murder... page 14

In the crime scene photos, the area around the safe is covered with blood, as is the front of the safe—but the inside of the safe is completely clean. Bowers was killed before the safe was open. It makes no sense that a robber would have shot him after gaining the combination but before he'd opened the safe, in case the door were not really unlocked. But his wife knew the combination already. When the story broke, the police arrested Ruth, and she eventually confessed. Furman was bankrupt, and they were facing destitution, so she drugged him, then staged a murder-robbery to try to claim on his insurance.

3. A Vexing Theft .... page 18

If the break-in occurred during the storm, the entry point ought to reflect that. Given the strong winds and torrential rain, you would expect to see staining on the windowsill and the carpet beneath the window, and it would be unusual for the windows to be left neatly half-open, rather than disordered. The windows would have kept banging, too. While the thief could have timed entry with a thunderclap easily enough, the windows would have been making noise persistently afterwards. It's far more likely that the theft occurred after the storm—when Eldora Watson was asleep, and the butler, Matthews, was on his own. Since the gardener was sure no one entered or left after the storm's end, Matthews is the only one who can be responsible. When Miss Miller and her friend confronted him, he confessed to having stolen it in a sudden fit of covetousness. He returned the necklace unharmed, and obediently left Eldora's employment without references.

4. Attack Among the Antiques .... page 21

Beauchamp swung a poker at the assailant, which he blocked with his forearm. At the very least, that's going to leave a significant bruise. Gerber, the former employee, is wearing a heavy jacket despite the heat. When Parnacki asked him to remove it, he immediately broke down and admitted to the robbery. His time working with Beauchamp had given him good knowledge of the best times to rob the store.

5. The Killing of Rachael Wightman

Rachael's cousin, Irvin, claimed that he was stuck on a bus during the time of the murder, but the buses were on general strike, so he must be lying. After Josh pointed this out to his police contact, Irvin was arrested, and quickly confessed. He'd been obsessed with his cousin for years, and had finally attempted to propose. Her horrified refusal had driven him over the edge.

 6. The Thief of Time

According to Farr's story, he was attacked, blindfolded, and then tied down to a chair. His assailant then made him open the safe—yet he also says he didn't escape the chair until later. So there's no way he can be telling the truth, and the only reason to lie is if he himself is the thief. Faced with the glaring error in his story, Farr confessed to the theft, which he had hoped to claim insurance for. Business had been somewhat slow recently, and he simply wanted more money.

 7. The Midwinter Ball

Adding alcohol to water lowers its freezing point. Even cheap scotch wouldn't start freezing until around -30°F. The supposed beggar was the gang's lookout, and still had the whistle with which he had warned them that the police were coming. He'd used the alcohol in his bottle to pour over himself, so that he smelled convincingly drunk, and then refilled it with water and a drop of colouring. He stayed behind to give incorrect directions to the police, so that the gang could make a clean escape. When the police took him in, he quickly agreed to give up his friends in return for only a minor charge. The relic, a necklace of Miss Miller's, and most of the other stolen goods were recovered, and with so much attention suddenly on the church, the Bishop quickly found funds for full repairs.

 8. The Lost City

Andrews is deeply tanned, even weathered, which fits with being in the desert for a period of time. But he claimed to have shaved just the day before, and if he had really just removed three months of thick beard, a large part of his face would have been noticeably paler. The paper ran the story without mentioning the discrepancy. A few days later, Andrews started trying to solicit a significant amount of funding for a return trip to the city. The *Sentinel* then ran a piece questioning the explorer's veracity and mentioning the issue with the beard, and Andrews vanished from the city the next morning.

 9. The Death of a Brother

Alfie says that he was approaching the house when he saw Bradley kick the stool away and hang himself. Bradley was in the attic, which, from what Nita says, is four stories up. Alfie was close to the front door, so looking up at a high window, all he'd see would be a small patch of ceiling right next to the window. Even if Bradley hung himself right in front of the window, he still wouldn't be able to see a stool unless the attic window was floor-length—at which point, the attic would hardly be dingy. In fact, it eventually became clear that Alfie was also courting Libby Norton, and was extremely jealous that Bradley was winning her heart. Alfie and Bradley got into an argument. Alfie confessed to strangling his friend, and then staging a hanging to disguise the murder.

10. Stolen Sapphires... page 43

It's Sunday, so there's no chance that a postman would be working. Even a moment's thought would make that clear, particularly to someone who doesn't walk as well as he used to. Confronted, Joey Whitson broke down readily, and confessed to the theft. Although he'd managed to disguise how flustered he was to find himself face to face with the inspector, he hadn't been able to think of a good lie. He'd gone up to check on Walter, realized that the ring was on the dresser, and decided to steal it. The ensuing scandal cost him his job.

11. The Swaggerty Murder .... page 47

Harmon Sands said "murders" when seeming to dismiss the idea of Clifton Smith's guilt, not "murder." With no announcements yet made, only the murderer knows that there's a second victim. Sands was arrested, and confessed to the killing. He was desperate to get Swaggerty's job, which he was in line for. He was motivated partly by ambition, but also because he owed some large gambling debts that he couldn't really afford at his current salary.

12. A Nascent Scandal .... page 51

It's October, and cold—cold enough that Vida needs blankets when she goes downstairs—but the ceiling fan is running. Parnacki turned the fan off, and discovered the negatives in a small envelope, stuck to the top of a blade with a wad of chewing gum.

Vida's boyfriend, John, was the blackmailer. He had been staging the room to look as if it had been searched, when Vida got home early. He panicked, and decided it was too dangerous to carry the negatives with him, in case she called the police immediately and he got picked up before being able to stash them somewhere safe. So he quickly fixed them to the top of the fan with his gum, turned it on to make the envelope less visible, and let himself down from the window. He figured that he could come over to console her the following evening, and retrieve them when she was distracted. As soon as Parnacki confirmed with Vida that John chewed gum, he became the primary suspect, and confessed almost immediately when the magnitude of his potential punishment was spelled out.

13. The Missing Earrings .... page 55

Wherever possible, plants turn towards the sun rather than away from it. The hibiscus is pointing in the wrong direction, so it must have been recently moved and put back incautiously. When the ladies checked, the earrings were underneath its pot.

 14. The Late Mr. Early .... page 58

Crowson's clothes are clean, but he claims to have been moving bales of hay around. If that were true, he'd be covered in little pieces of straw, even if he'd tried to wipe himself down. The other men are clearly used to coming into the kitchen without changing, so why is Crowson tidy? Realizing his error, he confessed. Fed up with being constantly bullied, Crowson snapped and killed Early. Afterwards, he changed into some spare clothes and threw the old, bloody ones in a sack, then stayed in the shed fretting over his actions.

 15. The Ice Room Murder .... page 62

Sam Moyes is feeling guilty about providing Howard with a tip that led to his death. Howard's body was discovered that morning, but Sam says that his guilt led him to light a candle in memory of Howard the day before—so he must have already known that Howard was dead. Under intensive questioning, Sam admitted to being on a Mob payroll to keep inconvenient stories quiet, and that he'd accepted a large sum of money to pass the phoney tip to his colleague. He was able to confirm that the hit happened on Friday night, and Howard's killer was identified and caught shortly afterwards.

 16. The Overton House .... page 66

Why is Marvin Overton hanging anything in the hours before new tenants take over his house? It's an odd gesture at best. Tellingly, he claims that he's covering up an old stain, despite having had the walls painted just a few days beforehand. With Miss Miller backing her up, Regina was able to persuade the police to send an officer to the house. He found a small plug of damp plaster behind the mirror which, on investigation, turned out to be a bullet hole. With his escape prevented, Marvin eventually confessed to shooting his wife the night before during a very heated argument. Her body was found under a newly dug flower-bed in the garden.

 17. Bullet to the Brain .... page 70

If Rodgers had shot himself through the back of the head—which would have required putting the pistol in his mouth before pulling the trigger—how could he have put the gun on the desk and folded his hands across his chest? It can only be a sloppily staged murder. The killer was eventually identified as Julian Ottinger, whose father Edwin had been hounded to (genuine) suicide by Rodgers the week before.

SOLUTIONS

Petunias are an annual flower, as Miss Miller herself pointed out. Annuals only live for one year, so there's no way one plant could keep providing seeds. Griffiths could plausibly be ignorant of that fact, but he claims that his sadly deceased floral expert friend explained the business value of having the plants live for years. No genuine horticulturalist, even an amateur one, would make that mistake.

Burl Tuck was not the intended victim. The supposed new client had come to the office to kill Lucius Ray. A gang boss needed a case that Ray was pursuing to go away. Unfortunately, the killer didn't realize he'd been shown to the wrong partner, so when Tuck took the meeting instead, the killer murdered him and attempted to confuse matters by—as he saw it—writing the victim's partner's name in blood as a final accusation. Josh passed his information along to his police contact, and the killer, a hired gun who'd used the same alias several times, was eventually convicted.

Tom Francis says that after he and his wife escaped the fire, she darted back into the house, and presumably back into the flaming living-room, where she was overcome. The carpet beneath her is clean, however, neither burnt nor ashy. That very strongly suggests that she was lying there on the floor before the room caught fire. Forensic examination revealed that her lungs contained no smoke or ash particles, making it certain that she was dead beforehand. Faced with this, Tom confessed to smothering her while she slept. He'd been having an affair, and had fallen deeply in love with the other woman. Rather than risk scandal, he decided to free himself by staging the tragic death of his wife in a fire.

Mayes is wearing pale clothing—with no hint of paint specks—but is quite firm that he came straight from painting his porch to sitting beside his wife's body. It's highly likely that he's either lying about painting the porch that morning, or about not having changed clothes. He later confessed to murdering his wife after an argument on their return from church. He staged the scene to look like an intruder, then went to do the painting that would establish his alibi. Once he'd raised the alarm, he absent-mindedly changed back into something more comfortable before going to wait for the police to arrive.

Given that the house was unusually silent, it is unlikely that the intruder used the French doors without alerting Annabel Voss. The kitchen doors might be possible to open quietly (or might not), but the build-up of cobwebs on the outside of the door suggests that it's been at least a couple of days since it has last been used. The front door would have alerted Annabel, according to her own statement. So the intruder must have come through the terrace door. As we're told it would have been impossible to get in through the ballroom without Arlene's knowledge, the implication is that she was in on it. She was later arrested for conspiracy, and gave up the kidnappers—her cousin was part of a small gang—in return for consideration in sentencing.

23. The Gunman...page 91

Peter Davey claims to have entered the liquor store by its side door, but that's impossible as there's a cabinet blocking the way. He must be lying, and the timing of the shots and the other men's attention strongly implies he could only have been in the store if he was the killer. When a gun was found in a dumpster outside his home, he confessed to robbing the store. He was in arrears on his shop rent, and desperate for money. He killed Tom to avoid being immediately identified.

24. The Investigation ....page 95

Everyone thinks that Forrest Lewis was shot, because of the gun. So how does Alfonzo Parker know that his head was beaten in? After his arrest, Parker confessed to killing Lewis—with a blackjack—and leaving the gun to confuse matters. He'd discovered that Lewis was having an affair with his wife, and the double betrayal was too much to bear.

25. The Golfer...page 98

Lonnie's alibi is based on the whistling kettle marking Faye as having been recently interrupted. But if the kettle had been set up significantly earlier, he would no longer have an alibi. The way to make sure that a kettle takes much longer to boil dry than it otherwise would do is to pack it full of ice, in this instance from the open icebox. Lonnie was rearrested, and when it came out that he was having an affair with the wife of a colleague, he broke down and confessed.

26. The Fabric Man...page 101

Koontz claims to have been at the match, but appears unaware that Petty, whose performance he spoke so highly of, didn't actually play. Faced with his lie, he quickly confessed to attacking Rule and stealing several consignments of expensive goods.

SOLUTIONS

27. The Vinson Scandal

Beauchamp describes the policeman as having brown eyes. However, earlier he says that the man is wearing dark glasses. Since he also states that the supposed thief comes out "just like before", he apparently didn't change his outfit. So there's no way he could have seen the man's eyes. The paper published the scoop anyway, along with an artist's illustration. The real thief was never caught.

28. The Mugging

Remember that the victim's broken watch was stolen. Delbert Calfee knows that the victim was physically assaulted, but thinks that the time is considerably earlier than it actually is. One of those might be a coincidence, but both together are quite damning. Faced with his mistakes, Calfee confessed to the mugging.

29. The Clockwork Owl

The bronze figure is dusty. According to the man's story, the owl was closed up in its metal box and wrapped in cloth when his great-grandmother died, where it stayed almost constantly until a very short while ago. How then has dust managed to collect inside the metal box? The most likely answer is that it was put there deliberately, to help give it an air of age. After some pointed questioning, and some equally pointed dickering, Zelma purchased the device for a tenth of the original asking fee—a fair price for a piece made in the last year or two.

30. The Hero

When they're making introductions, Allison knows that Josh can't shake hands, even though Josh hasn't said anything about it. In fact, Allison did still have some sight—not enough for full function, but sufficient to get by. The *Sentinel* didn't mention it, and if the other papers knew, neither did they. The little girl's father gave the man a job in the hotel he managed, which he then held successfully from then on.

31. Under Attack

The assailant, who attacked Philip from behind as he was leaving and then ran off, was facing away from the business the entire time. Monroe even confirmed that he never saw the man's face. So how did he know his tie was blue? Under questioning, Monroe admitted that the man had previously approached him and attempted to coerce him into selling the business for cash. Monroe was prepared to give in, but pointed out that Phillips never would, at which point he was warned to say nothing, and that the man would return soon. The assailant was never identified, and there were no further attempts to harm or menace either man.

32. A Politician's Tale

The politician was standing in front of a large, pristine mirror when someone supposedly fired a shot at him. Obviously he's unhurt, so where did the bullet go? It ought to have very badly damaged the mirror he was standing in front of, but it remains pristine. After a long discussion with Hickman's campaign manager, the editor of the *Sentinel*, Reuben Marley, decided to print Hickman's story as he'd told it.

 33. Robbery at Bisbury's

All four men have reasonable alibis for the evening at first glance, and despite the evident morale issues at the store, none of them says anything actively incriminating. Gene Reynolds is quite correct about the cow in the stage play of *The Wizard of Oz*. However, there is a chair immediately in front of the safe, where it would be more regular for a smallish office to have both visitor chairs in front of the desk. Only one of the staff members is short enough to possibly need a chair to get full access to the safe—Marius Morse. When the chair was pointed out, Morse started blustering, and was duly arrested on suspicion. He later confessed, and the stolen money was found under his bed. Thomas Lane was not sacked, but resigned anyway, and started a landscaping company.

 34. Murder in the Alley

The finer details of the crime are being kept quiet by the police for now, but Julian somehow knows that Antoinette's body was found in a dumpster. Josh tipped Pete off as soon as the story was ready to run, and by the following lunchtime, Julian had confessed to the murder. He had stopped at a late deli for a sandwich on the way home, and she had caught up with him. They were both tipsy, and as they headed back towards the area they both lived in, they got into an argument about when he was going to propose. He pushed her over angrily, and her head landed on a sharp corner, killing her. Panicking, he threw her body into a dumpster and ran off.

 35. The Root Cellar

The likelihood of someone finding a long-lost key and knowing both the house and door it belongs to is slim, considering that Rachel makes no mention of a label or tag attached to the key. Even more damningly, the key has supposedly been lost in the woods for months, but does not appear rusted or filthy. Under police questioning, Barry Ray admitted to having lied about losing the key. When the Colliers did not replace the lock, he sold the spare to a career criminal he knew casually. As part of that deal, he agreed to warn the team of upcoming occasions when he knew the Colliers would be out. Thanks to his cooperation, the whole group were arrested and eventually imprisoned, and Rachel got most of her belongings back.

36. The Banana Trade ....**page 137**

Reagan said that he went round the side of the bar into an alley. So how did he see Cochran murder Marks, who was near the front of the bar? Even if there were some line of sight through the bar windows—unlikely, given that the bar is dingy—there would be very little prospect of Reagan seeing enough of the actual pavement in front of the bar to identify blood coming from Marks's wound. Reagan eventually confessed to the murder. He had been approached by opium distributors who offered them the chance to graduate up from alcohol, but Marks had refused, threatening to go to the police if Reagan started smuggling drugs—so Reagan killed him.

 37. Death at Parrott's ....**page 141**

Johnny Brendan said he found Murphy's body with the axe in it a little after 10:45, as Felder & Sons were arriving. However, Gregory and his colleague Winston didn't return the axe to its home until almost 11:00. The discrepancy was enough to call Brendan's account into question, and when the police found the stolen Parrott's goods in a lock-up of Brendan's, he confessed. Murphy had found him stealing from the warehouse while everyone else was busy, so he killed the man, bopped himself on the head with the axe-handle, and pretended to have been out for a while. Unfortunately, he didn't know that the axe had been in use at the time he claimed to find the body.

 38. The Missing Specimen...**page 146**

Griffith makes a point of establishing a very solid alibi before anyone at the auction house has been informed that there was a break-in at Matthew's house the previous night. Why would he do that unless he already knew about it? After talking to Miss Miller, the police questioned Griffith, and he finally confessed to selling the name and address of the passenger pigeon's buyer to one of the failed bidders. Although the buyer didn't outright say he was going to steal the bird, Griffith was worried enough about the prospect to go out and make a spectacle of himself as an alibi. He wasn't charged, but he was fired, and the thief arrested.

 39. The Printer's Wife ....**page 150**

There are several off-notes in Dailey's story. For example, if he's at a trade fair 200 miles away, why is his secretary at work on Saturday morning? Why would the police think to contact his work on Saturday to try to inform him about his wife's death, rather than just leaving a message at home? But the temperature of the house is the most telling signal that Dailey is lying. He claims that he was turning the gas back on in the house when Inspector Parnacki knocked. It's frosty outside, yet inside, the house is warm. There's no way the place could have heated up so quickly. In fact, Dailey was in the basement making sure that the clothes he'd been wearing when he murdered his wife were fully burnt. He confessed under questioning to having become so resentful of the ongoing drain his wife presented to his income that he decided to just kill her. His story about the meeting was a sheer fabrication.

 ## 40. Death on the Steps...page 154

Max Stanton claims to have arrived after the group listening to Tarwater had dispersed in panic, yet he is able to state that the reason the gunshot wasn't audible is because of a truck going past. Acting on Josh's tip, the police interviewed Max Stanton at length, and eventually traced the gun that killed Tarwater back to his ownership. It turned out that Stanton had links to a rival of Benny Lucas. Macinello, a mob lieutenant, was a problematic target, but one of Lucas's lawyers made for a perfect reprisal for the murder Macinello had committed.

 ## 41. The Peacock Room...page 158

The carpet in the Peacock Room is soaking wet, so it must have been rained on—and the rain stopped around 8pm. So Zena's statement that the room was fine just before 9pm must be a lie. Faced with her error, Zena confessed to the police. While the family were eating, she went up to the room, broke the skylight with a broom and knocked the glass in, then stole the items and hid them at the bottom of a disused dresser in the spare bedroom.

 ## 42. Blackwell's Boiler Company ....page 162

Milicent Lewelling is extremely efficient, according to Zachary Harris. She's spent the morning running around obtaining a range of items for Joseph Keith's important meeting. So why, five minutes before the meeting starts—when she's clearly expecting the clients—are all the items she bought beside her desk rather than laid out in the meeting room? She knew that the meeting wasn't going to happen, because she was the one who killed Joseph Keith. Faced with the obvious, she confessed readily. He'd recently started becoming suspicious of her activities, and would shortly have put together proof that she had been steadily embezzling money from the firm's accounts for months. When Keith scheduled a meeting with Calderon and Justus, she saw a chance to get rid of him and have it blamed on the mob. So she passed him the note, saying she needed to talk, and when he joined her in the park, she stabbed him quietly, and slipped away.

 ## 43. Joiner's Hill..page 166

Both men were thrown clear of the crash. Morrison ended up on the pavement, impaled on a piece of metalwork, while Manning broke his leg. So why is there blood actually in the cab? It can only be because Morrison was in the cab when he was run through, and that means that Manning must have stabbed him. If the injury had occurred in the crash, Morrison would not have been flung clear. Under questioning, Manning confessed to murdering his friend as revenge, because the man had been having an affair with his wife. He sabotaged the cart so it would be easy to trigger it unhitching, then at the top of the hill, he stabbed Morrison with a piece of the material they were delivering, and set the cart loose. As they reached the bottom of the hill, he pushed Morrison out, and jumped out himself, trusting in the wreck to disguise his murder.

 44. Murder in Winter ....**page 169**

Raleigh Garland got home at 6.30pm, an hour and a half after the snow stopped. When Officer Pruitt arrived on the scene half an hour later, he had difficulty finding his way to the house because the snow had blanketed the path and there were no signs of where to walk. So how did Garland get from the street to his door? He must have been home before the snow stopped. Eventually, Garland admitted to murdering his wife. He ducked out of a large group meeting after making sure a few people had noticed him there, and came home early. Then he killed Madge, and opened the door (and the lounge windows) to cool the house off. He also took some valuables to make it look like a robbery, and hid them outside, in the snow. After a couple of hours, he closed the windows and called the police. He'd been having an affair with a glamorous twenty-seven-year-old, and wanted to be free to marry her.

 45. The Last Performance...**page 172**

If there was only one gun, and only one shot, then despite Nichols's insistence, the prop revolver must be the murder weapon—and the only person in a position to chamber a round was the prop manager, Foster Grey. He didn't turn up for work that evening, and when he was eventually found, he confessed to being blackmailed into loading the revolver with a live round. His situation was tangled—highly compromising photographs were involved—but he'd gone along with it because his blackmailer had promised (and then failed) to plant incriminating evidence on Luskan that would make him look guilty.

 46. The Widow ....**page 176**

Condensation forms when warm, damp air hits a cool surface. In the summer, it often forms on the outside of windows, after dawn. In winter, it forms on the inside of windows, and is most prevalent at night. As Mason pointed out, it was a cold night. There would have been no condensation outside to wipe off. Faced with his lie, he broke down and readily confessed. He'd called on Polly and tried to persuade her to leave Clark for him. They got into a heated argument, and he pushed her. She fell over and hit her head, which caused a fatal injury. Mason was eventually imprisoned for manslaughter.

47. The Audacious Burglar

Mack the gardener saw the intruder through the fountain, which blurred the man's face. Except that the fountain is electric, and the power was off. Mack must be lying, forgetting that the fountain wasn't working. Under questioning, the man confessed to inventing the intruder and committing the robbery himself, knowing that everyone else would be distracted by the dinner festivities.

 48. The Sloop Man

By the time the skin of a corpse has gone pale, the blood has settled, and dragging the body would not leave a trail of blood on the ground—particularly not when the entry wound is on the upper surface of the body. There would have been some smearing of the blood already spilled, but that would have thickened to the point where there would have been a few streaks, not a trail. Hayes must have moved Kenton soon after death, and the only reason to lie about the timing—and the pallor of the skin—would be if he were the murderer. He readily confessed when confronted. It transpired that Kenton had been in the process of romancing away Hayes's love, a woman named Marjorie Rennie. It was too much for Hayes to bear.

 49. The Insurance Salesman

Ganton claims to have had no idea that Simms was married, which implies that he habitually removed his wedding ring when around her. As evidenced by the corpse, however, he did not think to remove the ring when tanning. So when they met after his return, the tan-line of his wedding ring was obvious. Incensed, Ganton brought a gun to their next meeting, after work hours at his office, and shot him. The gun was found in her home later that day, and matched to the bullets taken from Simms's body. At that point, she confessed, and pleaded her rage at being so badly betrayed.

 50. The Boxton Liquor Store

Alex says that the robber entered at 9pm, and he didn't think anything of the man's presence at the time. But the main door is locked from 6pm, when Alex's shift started, so he should have been surprised and alarmed to see someone enter. Josh pointed out to Pete that Alex was almost certainly the thief, so he was hauled in for a night in the cells. The next morning, Alex was desperate to make amends for staging the theft. He was cautioned, but not prosecuted.

LEVEL 2

 1. The Gales

When Thelma got up and staggered a few paces after being stabbed, the droplets of blood that she trailed on the path were round. This means that the air must have been still, which places her time of death after 10pm, when the gale died down. We know from the body that she hadn't been in a scuffle, or forcibly restrained. So she must have left her uncle's house after the gale subsided—and not at 7pm, as the man insisted.

Eventually the knife was positively traced back to Victor, which secured a conviction. The man had become obsessed with his son growing up to be, as he saw it, "strong". Ewan was by nature gentle and artistic, but Victor blamed the influence of his wife for "corrupting" the boy. He killed her, and successfully made it look like suicide. But then Thelma took over with Ewan, and he still didn't get "stronger". Finally, he took the chance of Thelma's delay in leaving to talk to her about what he considered the problem of Ewan. She attempted to convince Victor that nothing was wrong, which just persuaded him that she needed to die. So he offered to walk her home after the storm, and murdered her *en route*.

 ## 2. The Star of Rajpur...page 203

All of the staff were alone at one point or another during the day, so it is more useful to ask why all the stones were prised out of the setting, both real and fake, but the valuable gold was left behind. Taking the extra time to do that considerably added to the risk. The most obvious reason is that the thief didn't actually know what he was after. Brady Ivey, who hadn't even heard of sapphires, was able to remember that the blue stone was valuable, but faced with the finished piece, he got overwhelmed and uncertain, and decided the only option was to take all the stones. But he wouldn't have come up with such a plan himself—if he had decided on his own that stealing the Star was a good idea, he would hardly have prised the stones out; he would have taken the whole thing. Even a fool knows gold is valuable. So it was someone else's plan.

But, as already ascertained, all the staff had opportunity. Even Acie had time alone after Mrs. Brookshire left for the night. The only reason to entrust the actual theft to a rather dim third party—increasing the risk over that of just taking it yourself during a quiet moment—is if you didn't have access yourself. Henri Rimel was the only other person who knew about the delivery. He desperately wanted to keep the Star, but didn't dare try to replace it with a fake copy when it would be surrounded by paste gems. Since Emmeline's whole point in commissioning the piece was to make the original stand out, a convincing fake would have been extraordinarily difficult to create.

So Rimel delivered the finished piece, and on the way out, decided to make use of Brady. He buttered the lad up, and talked him into retrieving the Star as a "funny joke," and meeting him at the gate to hand it over when he went up to the woodbin for logs. Brady fetched all the stones, to be safe, and Rimel just dumped the ones he didn't want. Then he turned on Brady, pointing out that the lad was now a major criminal, and brutally drilling it into his head that he was in huge, huge trouble, and his only hope was secrecy. To hammer home the point, he threatened Brady's family with savage violence if he ever mentioned Rimel's name.

Unfortunately for Rimel, Brady's taking all the stones and not the gold clearly pointed him out to Miss Miller, and made a third party's involvement clear. Following police surveillance, Rimel was caught trying to fence the Star to a shady private collector. Brady was neither charged nor sacked, but he did get a series of lessons from Collins on dealing with strangers and avoiding other obvious traps.

3. The Birdwatcher ....page 213

When Rebecca found Martin and screamed for help, the whole party rushed upstairs. When Miss Miller called her name, she jumped, and accidentally knocked the vase off its table, cracking it. The fact that nothing was stolen does strongly imply a personal attack against Martin, which in turn suggests one of the guests. It would be unnecessarily difficult and dangerous for an outside assailant to ambush Martin at a party full of people.

While Mike and Willis were carrying Martin downstairs, Miss Miller heard a latch click shut. The rest of the group should have been on the stairs already, but in the fuss, Miss Miller hadn't been paying particular attention to the group's composition, and neither had anyone else. If the assailant escaped through the open window upstairs, who closed a door behind the group with Martin?

When everyone in the group was accounted for after Rebecca had driven off, Miss Miller became suspicious that the attacker was a member of the party. Then, after the search, Mike reported having found a poker in the room with the open window. That made it virtually certain the attacker was not a panicked thief. Finally, he mentioned the broken vase, and David suggested that it might have been knocked over by the intruder. However, everyone in the group saw Rebecca knock it over when panicked.

David had become (incorrectly) convinced that Martin and Zettie were having an affair behind his back. Seeing them chat pleasantly at the party was the last straw. He followed Martin up to the bathroom, found the poker, and when Martin came out, he smashed him over the back of the head. Then he heard Rebecca coming up the stairs looking for her husband before he could sneak back down to the party, so he dropped the poker and hid in a cupboard in the small bedroom. He waited in there until he heard the assembled group head back downstairs, then slipped out of the small room and rejoined the group. Unfortunately for him, he had no idea that Rebecca had broken the vase, and that everyone else had seen her do it.

Miss Miller came back with a policeman, who took initial comments from everyone. In her interview, she made sure to point out to him that everyone had seen Rebecca break the vase, and when David was unable to explain his ignorance, he was arrested. Martin survived, and mostly recovered, save for some loss of function in his left arm. David was eventually imprisoned for attempted murder.

4. The Double Widow ....page 221

Matthew Cutshaw's timeline doesn't quite work. He says that he heard the glass break, and went to investigate. But he arrived slowly enough for Camilla to get out of the bath in response to the same noise, wrap herself up, find the body, check it, then sit down and go into a degree of shock for a while. The broken glass was outside, indicating the balcony wasn't how the killer got in. In addition, Yetta said that she heard the door before he called for assistance for Camilla, but that was supposedly before he apprehended Maxie. Camilla says that it took a few minutes for Cutshaw to return after dashing off, which is very little time to locate, subdue, restrain and lock up an intruder who could be anywhere in a large area of grounds.

This is because Cutshaw was the killer. He was totally infatuated with Camilla, and had convinced himself that her pleasantness toward him was subtle flirtation. He decided that she needed someone younger and more handsome than her husband, so he used an old army friend turned low-level criminal to pick a likely intruder in the form of Maxie, and arranged for him to receive a tip that the McMurray house would be empty that night, and very profitable to burgle. Then he kept an eye out, and when he spotted Maxie approaching the house to case it, he grabbed the man, tied him up, and locked him in the shed. With his suspect in place, he waited until Delmar was alone, killed him, broke the window, and dropped down from the balcony. Then he made his way back into the house to find the body, after which he dashed back outside, waited around a little, then returned to announce he'd caught Maxie.

Cutshaw eventually confessed, and was convicted.

5. The Golden Hind ....page 231

Buddy Cross got a little confused about what he saw, which was, after all, a momentary glimpse in a mirror. There was no note—it was the tattoo on the back of Rubin Wilson's right hand. Wilson entered the restaurant casually at around 9pm, when Merle Wheeler was away from the door, looking after customers. He sauntered through to the restrooms, and no one paid any attention. Then he waited until most people had left (and therefore paid) before putting on the mask and, once Murray Blevins was distracted, attacking him. He had in fact been to the restaurant a week or so earlier with a girlfriend, and used the opportunity to examine the layout. The exit to the alley behind the place was quite clear when waiters opened the door, coming out of the kitchen with food. When confronted with the gun and the mask, he confessed.

6. Uncle Edmond ....page 241

While any of the people at the house that weekend would have had plenty of motive to kill Edmond Pemmons, only one of them lied to her about their whereabouts—Myles. He told Miss Miller that after breakfast, he was in the old gallery watching the sun rise and enjoying a restorative moment of peace. However, when Miss Miller arrived at the house in the evening, the sun was setting through the old gallery windows. Having spent most of his adult life getting away from the house, Myles had forgotten that the old gallery showed the sun at dusk, not dawn. After Porter had been cut out of the will, Edmond warned Myles after breakfast that he was next if he didn't become more sober and respectable. It wasn't so much the thought of poverty as outrage which drove him to follow his father and stab him on the stairs. When Miss Miller spoke to McLemore and confirmed that he'd not seen anyone in the gallery after breakfast, but that Myles and Edmond had spoken, she confronted Myles about letting Porter die. Myles broke down, and confessed. Porter was freed, and while Myles spent some time in prison, it was not an especially onerous sentence.

 ## 7. The High-flyer ....page 250

Clem wasn't writing the word "HELP". He was writing the word "WILHELM", naming his killer. Along with part of the "H", the water had also washed away the letters "W", "I", and "L" entirely. Wilhelm had realized that his wife was cheating on him. He used the cover of his frequent trips to spy on her, and when he discovered that Clem was behind it, he decided to lay a trap. He sent a note in a handwriting close to his wife's, calling Clem out to the beach, and lay in wait. When Clem got out there, Wilhelm confronted him, and then killed him. The knife went into the sea. The police managed to show that Wilhelm had not been on the trip he claimed at the time, at which point he confessed. Once Josh had broken the story, Katherine appeared repeatedly in all of the papers, but then Wilhelm obviously already knew about her infidelity.

 ## 8. The Note ....page 260

Clark Payne was responsible for his own death. He knew that Evan would be away for a few days, so after pretending to go off on a business trip, he used his key to attempt to airproof Evan's lounge, prepared supplies for staging a fake suicide, and set the nitrogen canister in place. Having assembled everything, his intention was to come back the night before Evan's return, prepare the room, and set the timer on the canister for the next day. He then hoped to return after Evan's death but before the alarm was raised, and set the scene convincingly. Unfortunately for Clark, the timer malfunctioned, and he was overcome without realizing what was happening. The motive had nothing to do with his anaemic inheritance, however. Clark's mistress, "M", was Marianne Milton, his brother's fiancée. What was supposed to be a rebellious little fling had turned serious, and Clark was deeply in love. He couldn't persuade Marianne to leave Evan, so he convinced himself that if Evan appeared to commit suicide, she would turn to him.

9. The Heirloom Ring

Three elements are required to make a likely suspect in the theft of the ring—awareness of its existence, opportunity to retrieve it, and knowledge regarding which case belonged to Shelton Dole. As ornithologists, both Oliver Griffith and Elwood Hembry could possibly know Shelton's peewit-decorated case. Although Hembry was not at the ornithological society for long, his excellent memory ensured he remembered Shelton's bag. Of the two, only he left the conference. That identifies him as the likely thief.

Miss Miller helped Shelton persuade the police to start by investigating Hembry, and after a minimal amount of questioning, he broke down and confessed to stealing the ring and passing it to his wife when she met him during the afternoon. It was recovered from his house, and returned to Shelton. Hembry was in significant financial trouble following some very unwise wagering on chess games he played against a skilled grifter, and the ring seemed like a perfect way out.

10. Anastasia

When she was strangled, Anastasia was in the process of dyeing her hair. There was enough of a struggle for hair dye to end up on the walls. Therefore it's almost certain that there would have been dye stains on the killer's hands, and while they can be faded with some effort, they are very difficult to eliminate completely. Of the suspects, Gustavo Schultz is the only one who is wearing gloves. When Inspector Parnacki called Schultz back and asked him to remove his gloves and hold his hands under a fluorescent bulb, the man immediately demanded a lawyer. Despite his best efforts, his hands were examined, and traces of Anastasia's hair dye were found. These proved sufficient, in the end, to secure a murder conviction. Despite his protestations, Schultz had become fed up of the amount of money that Anastasia was costing him, and rather than risk her making good on her threats to damage his career with public denouncements, he decided to kill her.